PILLOWS, CURTAINS & SHADES
step by step

PILLOWS, CURTAINS & SHADES
step by step

DK

Penguin Random House

DK PUBLISHING
Project Editor Anne Hildyard
Senior Art Editors Saskia Janssen, Kathryn Wilding
Managing Editors Lisa Dyer, Angela Wilkes, Lori Hand
Senior Managing Art Editor Marianne Markham
Jacket Designers Nicola Powling, Amy Keast
Producer, Pre-Production Andy Hilliard
Producer Niamh Tierney
Art Director Maxine Pedliham
US Publisher Mike Sanders
Publisher Mary-Clare Jerram

DK INDIA
Project Editor Arani Sinha
Art Editor Sourabh Challariya
Assistant Art Editor Juhi Sheth
Deputy Managing Editor Bushra Ahmed
Managing Art Editor Navidita Thapa
Pre-Production Manager Sunil Sharma
DTP Designer Rajdeep Singh

First American Edition, 2017
This edition published in the United States in 2017 by
DK Publishing, 345 Hudson Street, New York, New York 10014

Copyright © 2017 Dorling Kindersley Limited
DK, a Division of Penguin Random House LLC
17 18 19 20 21   10 9 8 7 6 5 4 3 2 1
001 – 286835 – Feb/2017

Material in this publication was first published in
the U.S. and Great Britain in *Handmade Interiors* (2015)

All rights reserved.
Without limiting the rights under the copyright reserved above, no
part of this publication may be reproduced, stored in or introduced
into a retrieval system, or transmitted, in any form, or by any means
(electronic, mechanical, photocopying, recording, or otherwise),
without the prior written permission of the copyright owner.
Published in Great Britain by Dorling Kindersley Limited

A catalog record for this book is available from the Library of Congress.
ISBN 978-1-4654-5575-8

Printed and bound in China.

All images © Dorling Kindersley Limited
For further information see: www.dkimages.com

A WORLD OF IDEAS:
SEE ALL THERE IS TO KNOW

www.dk.com

Contents

HOME DECOR SEWING

Sewing machine

A sewing machine will speed up any sewing job. Most of today's machines are aided by computer technology, which enhances stitch quality and ease of use. Always try a sewing machine before you buy, to really get a feel for it.

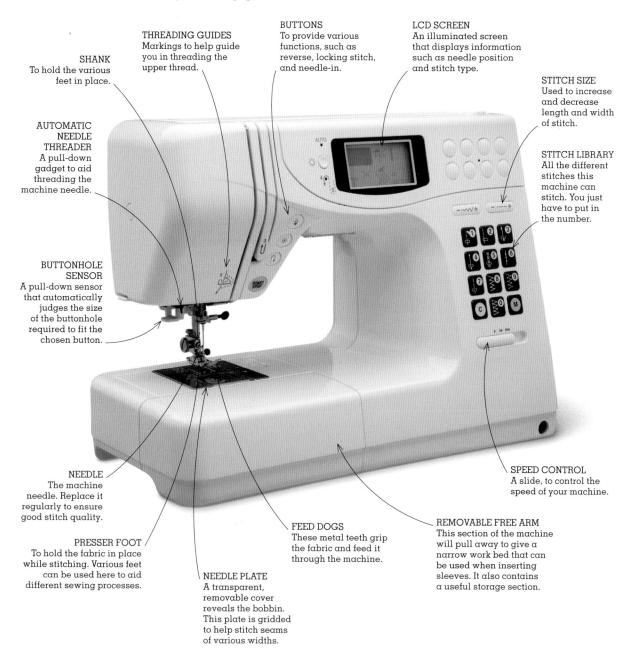

THREADING GUIDES
Markings to help guide you in threading the upper thread.

BUTTONS
To provide various functions, such as reverse, locking stitch, and needle-in.

LCD SCREEN
An illuminated screen that displays information such as needle position and stitch type.

SHANK
To hold the various feet in place.

STITCH SIZE
Used to increase and decrease length and width of stitch.

AUTOMATIC NEEDLE THREADER
A pull-down gadget to aid threading the machine needle.

STITCH LIBRARY
All the different stitches this machine can stitch. You just have to put in the number.

BUTTONHOLE SENSOR
A pull-down sensor that automatically judges the size of the buttonhole required to fit the chosen button.

NEEDLE
The machine needle. Replace it regularly to ensure good stitch quality.

SPEED CONTROL
A slide, to control the speed of your machine.

PRESSER FOOT
To hold the fabric in place while stitching. Various feet can be used here to aid different sewing processes.

FEED DOGS
These metal teeth grip the fabric and feed it through the machine.

REMOVABLE FREE ARM
This section of the machine will pull away to give a narrow work bed that can be used when inserting sleeves. It also contains a useful storage section.

NEEDLE PLATE
A transparent, removable cover reveals the bobbin. This plate is gridded to help stitch seams of various widths.

Serger

A serger, or overlocker, is not necessary for making the projects in this book, but it is a useful, time-saving tool for neatening seams and other raw edges (see p.17). It provides a clean, professional finish by "serging" or "locking" the edge with a medium-length (3- or 4-thread) stitch that prevents the fabric from fraying. At the same time as making the serger stitches, it cuts away the surplus fabric from the edge using its built-in knives. You will still need a sewing machine to join the fabric pieces, but a serger, although pricey, will give your work a clean finish.

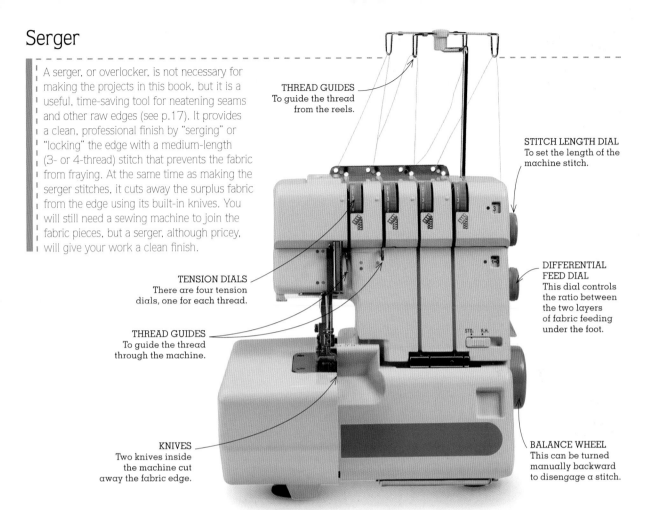

THREAD GUIDES
To guide the thread from the reels.

STITCH LENGTH DIAL
To set the length of the machine stitch.

DIFFERENTIAL FEED DIAL
This dial controls the ratio between the two layers of fabric feeding under the foot.

TENSION DIALS
There are four tension dials, one for each thread.

THREAD GUIDES
To guide the thread through the machine.

KNIVES
Two knives inside the machine cut away the fabric edge.

BALANCE WHEEL
This can be turned manually backward to disengage a stitch.

Sewing machine feet

The machine foot "runs" over the fabric, holding it in place while you are stitching. There are several types of specialized feet that can be used for different tasks. For the projects in this book, you will need the all-purpose foot, as well as a zipper foot and a buttonhole foot.

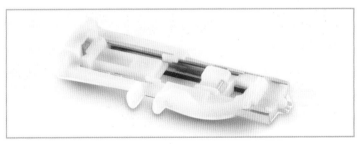

A zipper foot allows you to sew close to the zipper's teeth. It attaches to the left or right of the needle, according to the side of the zipper you are sewing.

A buttonhole foot enables you to stitch a perfectly sized buttonhole. You slip a button in the holder at the back of the foot, attach the foot to your machine, lower the machine's buttonhole lever, and stitch to complete.

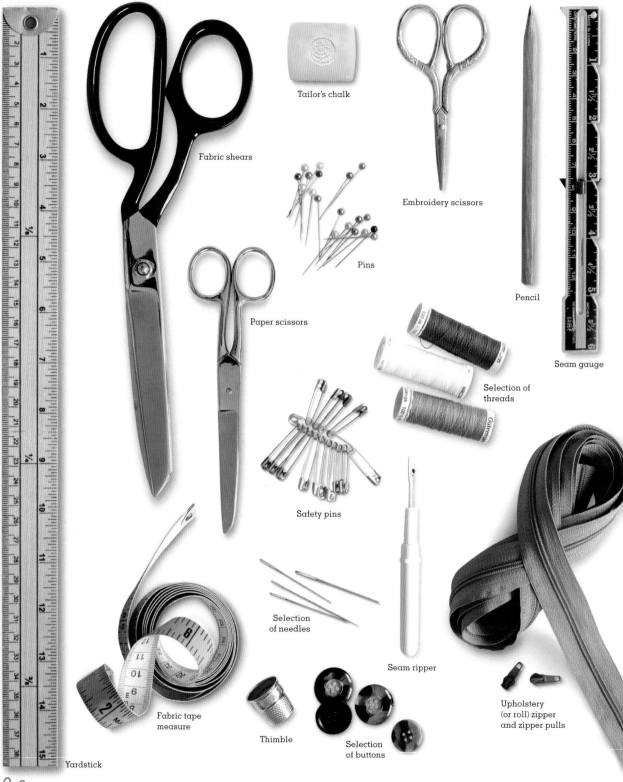

Fabric shears

Tailor's chalk

Embroidery scissors

Pins

Pencil

Paper scissors

Selection of threads

Seam gauge

Safety pins

Selection of needles

Seam ripper

Fabric tape measure

Thimble

Selection of buttons

Upholstery (or roll) zipper and zipper pulls

Yardstick

Home decor sewing

Essential sewing kit

A sewing machine is key to making the projects in this book, but you will also need other tools and accessories to cut, measure, mark, and pin fabric, as well as for the finishing touches required to create professional-quality items. Your basic sewing kit should include the items shown here, most of which are not very costly. You can add extra tools and equipment gradually as you undertake more complex projects.

CUTTING TOOLS

You will need a variety of cutting tools for different purposes, but one rule applies to all: buy good-quality equipment that can be resharpened. It is also advisable to keep a separate pair of scissors for cutting paper templates: that way you will not blunt your fabric shears by using them to cut paper. A seam ripper saves time when unpicking seams and removing basting stitches. Useful cutting tools include:

- Fabric shears
- Paper scissors
- Embroidery scissors
- Trimming scissors
- Thread snips, or clippers (for quickly cutting off the ends of your thread)
- Seam ripper
- Pinking shears

MEASURING TOOLS

No sewing kit is complete without the correct tools for accurate measuring. Keep these tools on hand for measuring fabrics and seam allowances, as well as finished lengths as you make up each project. Useful measuring tools include:

- Fabric tape measure
- Yardstick or short ruler
- Seam gauge

MARKING AIDS

The trick to marking fabric is to find a way of making marks that show up when you are assembling your project, but can be removed easily once the item is complete. Tailor's chalk comes in many different colors, is easy to remove, and can be used on all types of fabric. Water-soluble pens are good for accurate marking and can be removed by spraying the fabric with water. Ordinary pencil can be used in places where the marks won't show. Always test your marking tool—and whether you can remove the marks—on a scrap of fabric before you start, and be careful never to press over the marks, since this may set them permanently.

NEEDLES AND PINS

Using the correct pin or needle for your work is extremely important because the wrong choice can damage fabric or leave small holes, so always have a selection on hand. Keep them in good condition by storing pins in a pincushion and needles in a needle case. Pins and needles to buy include:

- A selection of "sharps" in sizes 6–9
- Milliner's, or straw, needles
- Glass-headed pins
- Dressmaker's pins
- Safety pins

THREADS

There are many types of thread to choose from. Polyester thread is the most popular, since it has a slight "give" and is suitable for sewing almost all fabrics. Cotton thread is firm and strong, while silk thread can be removed without leaving a mark, making it a good choice for basting. Always use silk thread for sewing silk fabric. Threads to buy include:

- Polyester all-purpose thread
- Cotton thread
- Silk thread

FASTENINGS

The projects in this book require a variety of different fastenings. Hook-and-loop tapes, such as Velcro tape, are used on projects such as blinds, to attach the blind to the batten. Upholstery zipper is particularly versatile, since it can be cut to the exact length required. Buttons can be used for closing pillow covers as well as for decoration. Useful fastenings to buy include:

- Velcro tape
- Upholstery (roll) zipper and zipper pulls
- Buttons in various sizes
- Metal self-cover buttons

USEFUL EXTRAS

There are many other items that make sewing easier. These include:

- Thimble
- Needle threader
- Tweezers

Home decor fabrics

These days there is an impressive selection of fabrics in stores and online, so it's no wonder many people are choosing to make home furnishings that reflect their own unique taste and style. From different widths, weights, and fibers, to almost endless pattern and texture options, read on to discover more about the wide range of home decor fabrics that are available.

Widths

Most home decor fabrics are made in 52¾in (132cm), 54¾in (137cm), or 56in (140cm) widths, with sheers made much wider at 3¼yd (3m). The width is measured from selvage to selvage, not including the width of the selvage itself. The width is usually marked on the bolt of fabric, but if in doubt, ask the retailer.

Weight

Fabrics are normally classified as being lightweight, medium-weight, or heavyweight, but you might occasionally hear the weight described according to the number of ounces per square yard or grams per square meter.

Drape—the way a fabric hangs—and weight should not be confused. You can have a heavyweight fabric that drapes well, while a lightweight fabric can be stiff and starchy. For curtains, you would normally look for a fabric that drapes well, while drape is not usually important for furniture covers.

Generally, the heavier a fabric, the more durable it is, but durability is also influenced by factors such as the fibers the fabric is made from and how tightly they are woven together. Most soft furnishings use light- to medium-weight fabrics, with heavyweight fabrics used more often for slipcovers. Note that heavyweight fabrics are usually bulky so they can be difficult to work with.

Common fibers

COTTON

Cotton is one of the most common home decor fabrics, thanks to its versatility, durability, and ease of care. It comes in different weights, weaves, and finishes, as well as in any number of prints. You can use it for everything from curtains and pillows to bedding and accessories.

WOOL

Wool is resilient and durable and it holds its shape well. It also resists wrinkles and dirt and is a good insulator. It can be used for almost any home furnishings, whether curtains, pillows, or slipcovers.

LINEN

Produced from the flax plant, linen works well for items such as curtains and pillows, but it does have a tendency to wrinkle. You can find it in different weights, weaves, and prints. Washed linen is great for a vintage look.

SILK

This luxurious fabric is produced by silkworms. It has a natural sheen, is strong, and has good insulation properties. It looks beautiful made up into curtains but since it can be damaged by sunlight, it is best to use an interlining, which will also make the curtains look fuller and even more luxurious. Silk can also be used for pillows, lampshades, and other items not subject to much wear.

SYNTHETIC

These fabrics are woven from man-made fibers rather than natural ones. Examples of synthetic fabrics include polyester, nylon, acrylic, and rayon. Synthetic and natural fibers are often blended together to produce fabrics that have the best qualities of each fiber.

PRINTS, PATTERNS, AND TEXTURE

Printed linen
Linen absorbs dye well so lends itself perfectly to a wide range of prints.

Linen blend
For greater resistance to wrinkling, linen can be blended with other fibers.

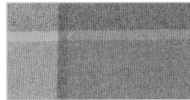

Wool-blend plaid
Wool mixed with cotton makes a durable plaid for home furnishings.

Velvet
Whether silk or synthetic, pay attention to the nap of velvet when cutting out.

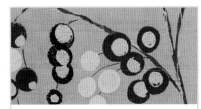

Printed silk
Silk absorbs dye well. It looks especially attractive with delicate prints.

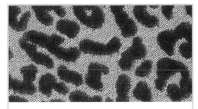

Textured synthetic
Velvet embellishments in the fabric give an interesting pattern and texture.

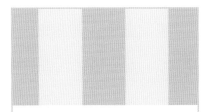

Cotton stripes
Stripes are classic. Pick a width that is in proportion to the item you are making.

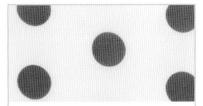

Cotton-blend polka dots
Polka dots on a polyester-cotton blend are a good choice for children's rooms.

Cotton-blend chevron
Chevrons are a bold but trendy choice. Try them on curtains and pillows.

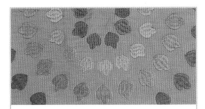

Embroidered embellishments
Embroidered embellishments add pattern, texture, and richness.

Appliqué embellishments
Appliqué motifs are another way of adding texture, color, and pattern.

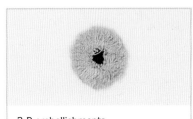

3-D embellishments
These may require special care, so don't use on items subject to heavy wear.

Using fabric

Checking fabric before you buy and cutting it out correctly are essential. Look for flaws, such as a pattern that's been printed off kilter or a faulty weave. Once you're home, check that the fabric has been cut from the roll at a right angle to the selvage. If it hasn't, start by squaring the edge.

Calculating fabric requirements

How much fabric you will need for an item will vary depending on the fabric you choose, how wide it is, and the pattern repeat. Here are some tips to get you started.

- Determine the width of the fabric. Many home decor fabrics come in standard widths of 54¾in (137cm) or 60in (150cm), but always double-check, since fabric widths can vary.
- Take into account the pattern and nap of the fabric. If you need to match a pattern repeat, this will require more fabric, and the larger the repeat, the more fabric you will need. "Nap" can refer to the pile of a fabric—the way it "shadows" when it is smoothed in one direction—or to a one-way pattern or uneven stripes. If your fabric has a nap, you should buy extra.
- Whenever possible, make a paper pattern first, then lay it out properly on your work surface, factoring in any pattern repeat

and nap. This gives you a pretty accurate guide to how much fabric you should buy.
- Always take into account shrinkage and fraying. If you plan to wash the item in the future, it is advisable to prewash the fabric so that any shrinkage occurs before cutting. And if the fabric is prone to fraying, buy a little more.
- In any event, always buy some extra fabric. If you make a mistake or a miscalculation, you may not be able to find more of the same fabric from the same bolt. Similarly, dye lots can vary from bolt to bolt, so you may not get an accurate color match if you have to buy more fabric later.

FABRIC GRAIN

Always cut out your fabric on the correct grain to ensure it will hang correctly without twisting. The grain is the direction in which the yarns or threads of a woven fabric lie. Mostly, you must cut parallel to the warp threads, or lengthwise grain. For some of the projects in this book, you will actually mark the straight of grain symbol (an arrow) on your pattern pieces.

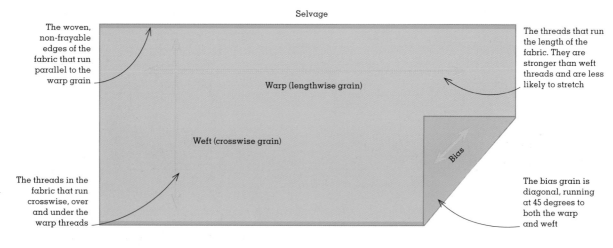

Selvage

The woven, non-frayable edges of the fabric that run parallel to the warp grain

The threads that run the length of the fabric. They are stronger than weft threads and are less likely to stretch

Warp (lengthwise grain)

Weft (crosswise grain)

Bias

The threads in the fabric that run crosswise, over and under the warp threads

The bias grain is diagonal, running at 45 degrees to both the warp and weft

LAYING OUT A PATTERN

In addition to paying attention to fabric grain (see above) when laying out your pattern pieces, you must also consider whether you need to cut one fabric piece from a single layer of fabric, two matching pieces from a double layer, or one symmetrical piece cut on the fold from doubled fabric. If using patterned fabric, be sure to consider pattern placement, too, so that motifs can be centered on an item or so that a pattern matches across two joined pieces.

MARKING AND CUTTING OUT

Mark your pieces using a water-soluble pen or tailor's chalk. The easiest way to measure and cut your fabric is to lay it out on a smooth, flat surface. If you do not have a large enough table, you may find it easiest to work on the floor. When cutting out, make sure you use a sharp pair of fabric scissors. And remember, always measure twice to cut once!

Using a triangle
You can use a large triangle to straighten the edge of a fabric. Align one perpendicular edge of the triangle with the selvage, then mark along the other perpendicular edge. Cut along the line.

Using the edge of a table
Start by aligning the selvage with the long side of a table. Allow the cut end of the fabric to overhang the end of the table. Run chalk along the edge to mark a line, then cut along the line.

Pulling a thread
On a loose-weave fabric you can use a pulled thread to get a straight edge. Snip into the selvage, find one single thread, and tug gently to pull it out. Carefully cut along the line left by the thread (inset).

ADDING A SEAM ALLOWANCE

A seam allowance is the area between the edge of a piece of fabric and the stitching line. For some of the projects in this book, you add the seam allowance to the pattern piece itself. In others, you add and mark it on the fabric. Here's how.

1 Lay the fabric face down with the pattern piece on top. Checking the project instructions, use a ruler to measure the length of the seam allowance from the edge of the pattern. Mark this distance at intervals along the pattern edge, then join up the marks to draw a solid line. This is your cutting line.

2 Before removing the pattern piece from the fabric, transfer any notches or other markings from the pattern piece to the fabric. Also mark any corners with a dot. Since you should not sew through a seam allowance, these dots will act as guides for where to start and stop stitching your seam.

Machine stitches

Your sewing machine will really come into its own as you make up the projects in this book. Here we show the types of stitches you will need, and introduce you to seam allowances.

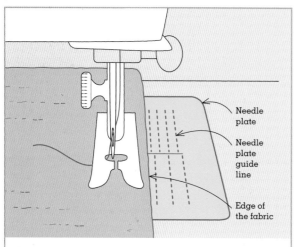

Needle plate

Needle plate guide line

Edge of the fabric

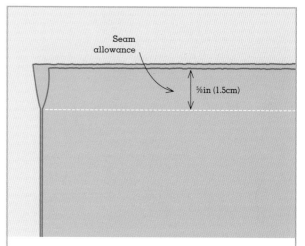

Seam allowance

⅝in (1.5cm)

STRAIGHT STITCH

The straight stitch is your sewing machine's default stitch setting. You will use it in most situations and for most fabrics. You can alter your stitch length to suit the type of seam and fabric using your machine's stitch length selector. For most seams and fabrics, use stitch length 2, but for decorative work, such as topstitching (see below), switch to stitch length 3. Some machines use visuals to indicate stitch length, rather than numbers.

SEAM ALLOWANCE

This is the distance between your line of stitching and the edge of the fabric. You should use the guide lines on your machine's needle plate to ensure that you keep the seam allowance constant as you work. Take care to always align the edge of your fabric along the same guide line. The size of the seam allowance will depend on the project you are working on, but in most cases it will be ⅝in (1.5cm).

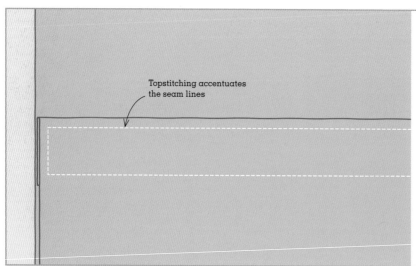

Topstitching accentuates the seam lines

TOPSTITCHING

This stitch holds layers of fabric together, which makes it a functional stitch, but since it is worked on the right side of the fabric, where it accentuates the seam line, it is also decorative. In certain situations, you topstitch using contrasting, sometimes thicker, thread and an even longer stitch, to accentuate the seam line more.

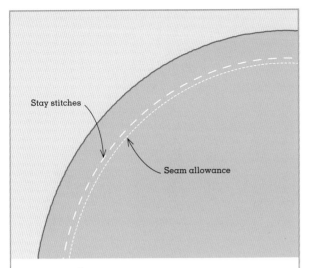

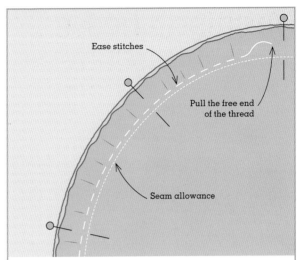

STAY STITCH

You will often use a line of stay stitches between the seam allowance and the curved raw edge of a single thickness of fabric. Stay stitches reinforce the curved edge, reducing the chances of the curve stretching or twisting before the fabric is attached to another piece. Stay stitches will not be visible on the finished item.

EASE STITCH

These are used when you need to fit an edge to an edge that is shorter, for example, when joining two pieces along a curve. Using a long stitch, simply sew a line of stitching within the seam allowance. Backstitch at the start but leave the end free. Pull the free end to gather the fabric gently until the edges of the two pieces of fabric match.

Neatening fabric edges

Once you have cut a piece of woven fabric, the edges will start to fray—and loosely woven fabrics fray very quickly. To prevent fraying, neaten the edges using one of the techniques shown below before you begin to construct the item. To save time, neaten all the edges together when you have cut out all the pieces.

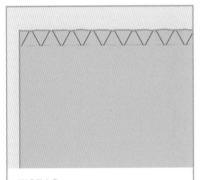

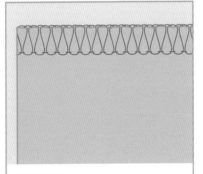

ZIGZAG

All sewing machines have a zigzag stitch. It is suitable for use on any fabric but you should adjust the width and length according to the fabric.

SERGING

This stitch requires a serger or overlocker (see p.9) and is the most secure way to neaten a fabric edge. There are both 3- and 4-thread serger stitches, although the former is more common.

PINKING

Pinking is the quickest and easiest means of neatening an edge, although loosely woven fabrics still fray somewhat after pinking. Simply cut along the fabric edge using pinking shears.

Hand stitches

Although most of your sewing for the projects in this book will be done by machine, there are times when stitching by hand will achieve the best results. Examples are when you are finishing curtain hems or attaching interlinings. Here are the hand stitches you will need for success every time.

PROFESSIONAL RESULTS

Using the correct hand-stitching techniques for each project ensures you achieve a professional finish. Practice stitching on spare pieces of fabric until you are confident that you have mastered the techniques.

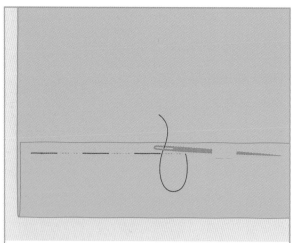

BASTING STITCH

Use basting stitches to securely hold two or more pieces of fabric in place before machine stitching them together. It is best to baste in a contrasting color; this makes it easier to see and remove the basting stitches once the seam is complete.

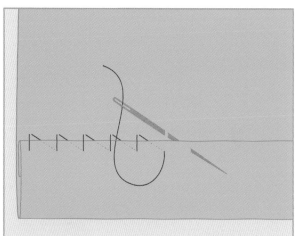

SLIP STITCH

Slip stitch is a useful hem stitch since the stitches do not show on the right side. It is also commonly used to close the opening on an item that has been machine stitched on the wrong side, then turned to the right side through the opening, for instance when making a fixed cushion cover (see the Round pillow, pp.62–69). When finished, the stitches will be hidden inside the seam.

INVISIBLE STITCH

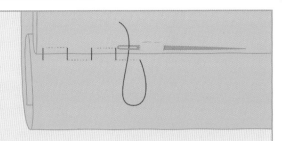

1 An invisible stitch is used to join two folded edges, as when joining the lining to an interlined curtain. Start by inserting the needle into one thickness of fabric, close to the fold. Pass it horizontally inside the fold, then bring it out again.

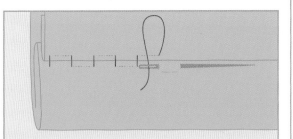

2 Now take the needle vertically across the fold. Insert the needle into the other fold, in the same way as before. Pass it inside the fold and out again. Repeat to complete the seam. Only the tiny vertical stitches will show, forming a "ladder" across the seam line.

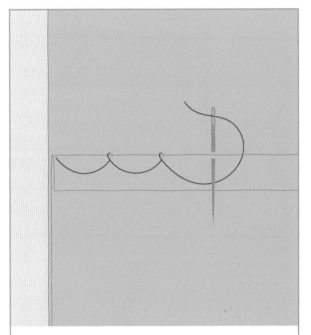

LOCKED WHIPSTITCH

A locked whipstitch is used to anchor or "lock" the interlining fabric to the main fabric when making an interlined curtain. Take care only to stitch through a few threads of the main fabric so the stitches don't show on the right side. Start by taking the needle through the folded edge of the interlining, then catch just a few threads of the main fabric with the needle, allowing the thread to form a loop across the interlining. Take the needle inside the loop, then through the folded edge of the interlining again. Repeat to complete the seam.

HERRINGBONE STITCH

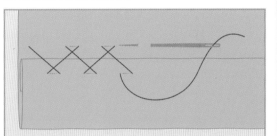

1 A herringbone stitch is a very secure stitch for a hem and for attaching interlinings. Working from the left, start by taking a short horizontal stitch from right to left, on one side of the fold.

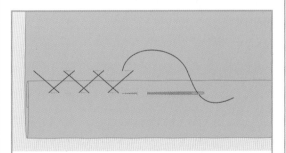

2 Pull the thread through, then take the needle diagonally across the fold and take another short stitch from right to left. Repeat to complete the hem.

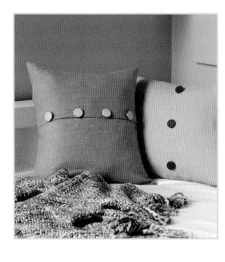

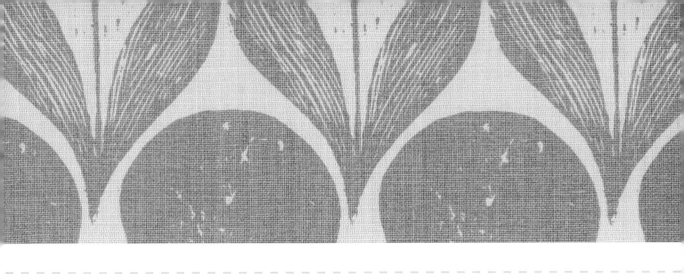

PILLOWS

Making pillows

When we talk about making pillows, we really mean pillow covers. Start by buying a synthetic or feather-filled pillow pad, then use the magic of sewing to create the perfect cover. The projects in this book will teach you how and will inspire you to design your own.

Calculating fabric

The starting point for calculating how much fabric you need for a pillow cover is always the dimensions of your pillow pad. If you like a plump pillow—and who doesn't?—make the cover to the same measurements as the pad. You do not need to add seam allowances; that way the pad will fit snugly inside the cover. If you're not sure of the dimensions of a pad you already have, measure it from seam to seam.

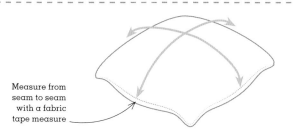

Measure from seam to seam with a fabric tape measure

Closures for your pillows

Some pillow pads are simply inserted through an opening in an envelope cover. The opening can be left open, in which case it is purely utilitarian and will be at the back of the cover, or it can be closed with decorative buttons at the front. Most of the pillow cover projects in this book, though, are closed with a zipper.

ROLL ZIPPER

If the zipper for your pillow cover is not a standard length, an upholstery, or roll, zipper will come to your rescue. Cut the zipper a bit longer than you need. The zipper pull comes separately and must be added before you sew the zipper in place.

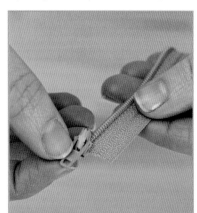

1 With one side of the zipper tape in one hand, insert the teeth into the corresponding side of the zipper pull with the other.

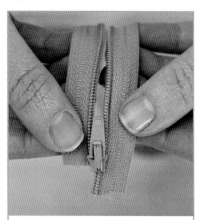

2 Draw the zipper pull about ¼in (5mm) along the teeth. Insert the other side of the tape into the other side of the zipper pull.

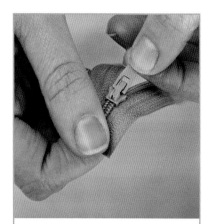

3 Draw the zipper pull along until it catches the teeth on both sides of the tape.

Types of pillows

Pillows are generally square, rectangular, round, or bolster-shaped. Round and square pillows work well as seat cushions, while bolsters are traditionally used on a bed or at either end of a sofa or daybed. Mixing and matching pillow shapes, sizes, closures, fabrics, and embellishments will add the wow factor to any room decor theme.

ENVELOPE

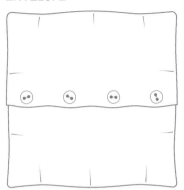

ZIPPERED

OXFORD

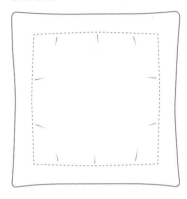

ROUND

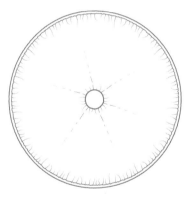

BOLSTER

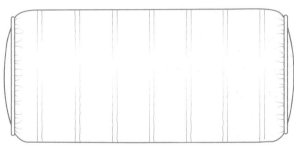

Decorative pillow fronts

Inject personality into your pillows by joining striped fabric panels to create a mitered front, by using panels of varying widths and fabrics, or by adding tucks. You can also use buttons, piping, and other trims (see p.58).

MITERED

PANELED

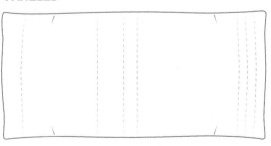

TUCKED

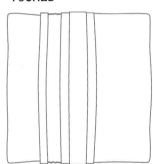

Envelope pillow

One of the simplest pillow covers to sew, an envelope cover can be made with or without buttons. The traditional version often has the closure at the back, but these zany contrasting buttons on a neatly tailored band make the closure on the front of the pillow the star attraction.

YOU WILL NEED

MATERIALS
- 18 x 18in (45 x 45cm) pillow pad
- 20in (50cm) light- or medium-weight home decor fabric
- Matching thread
- 4 x 1¼in (3cm) buttons

TOOLS
- Scissors
- Ruler
- Tailor's chalk
- Pins
- Iron
- Sewing machine
- Buttonhole foot
- Seam ripper

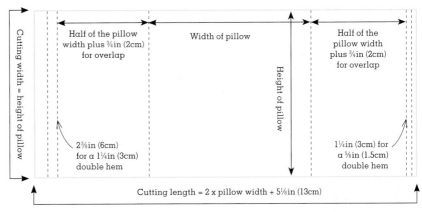

Cutting width = height of pillow

Half of the pillow width plus ¾in (2cm) for overlap

Width of pillow

Half of the pillow width plus ¾in (2cm) for overlap

Height of pillow

2⅜in (6cm) for a 1¼in (3cm) double hem

1¼in (3cm) for a ⅝in (1.5cm) double hem

Cutting length = 2 x pillow width + 5⅛in (13cm)

Determining the measurements
These instructions are for a pillow pad that is 18in (45cm) square. You can use the diagram above to figure out the measurements for a pillow pad of your choosing.

Cutting out and marking

Center point

Join the points on both sides of the center with a chalk line

To make an envelope cover for an 18 x 18in (45 x 45cm) pillow pad, cut a fabric rectangle 42⅜in (106cm) by 18in (45cm). On the wrong side, lightly mark the center point of one long edge with tailor's chalk, then mark 9in (22.5cm) to the right and 9in (22.5cm) to the left. Repeat along the other edge, then join these points with chalk lines. This gives the outline of the pillow back.

Making the hems

1 With the wrong side face up, turn over 1¼in (3cm) along one of the short edges and press. Turn over another 1¼in (3cm) and pin. Using medium-length stitch, sew in place. Add a line of topstitching (see p.16) as close to the outer folded edge as possible.

2 Turn over and press ⅝in (1.5cm) along the other short edge, then turn over another ⅝in (1.5cm) to create a double hem. Pin and machine stitch as before. Press to set the stitches.

Adding buttons and buttonholes

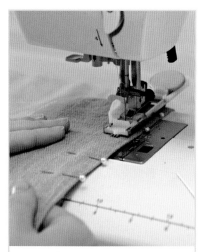

1 Fold the fabric along the marked lines, wrong sides together, so the 1¼in (3cm) hem is on top. Place the buttons on this hem, spacing them out by eye. Make sure that the outer buttons aren't too close to the edges.

2 Measure between the buttons to ensure they are evenly spaced and adjust if necessary. Place pins on each side of the buttons. These mark the position of the buttonholes.

3 Unfold the fabric. Using a buttonhole foot and following the manufacturer's instructions, machine stitch each buttonhole, starting at the pin that is closest to you. Remove the pins as you go.

4 Reposition a pin at each end of a buttonhole. Insert a seam ripper at one pin and push it forward to the next pin to open the buttonhole. Repeat for the other buttonholes.

5 Refold the fabric along the marked lines so that the buttonholes overlap the ⅝in (1.5cm) hem. Fold back the buttonhole hem and mark the center of each buttonhole with a pin on the narrower hem. Attach the buttons at the marked points.

Assembling the pillow

Pin the raw edges together and then stitch to finish the pillow cover

Unfold the fabric, then refold it, right sides together at the chalk lines and so that the edge with the buttons lies on top of the edge with the buttonholes. Pin the raw edges together, then stitch with a ⅝in (1.5cm) seam allowance. Turn the pillow cover to the right side and push the corners out. Press, then insert a pillow pad and fasten the buttons.

Zippered pillow

Both sides of this stylish pillow can be used as the front, thanks to an invisible zipper inserted into the bottom seam. Make it using two fabrics in different colors or textures to create a clever two-in-one pillow, or to showcase an extra-special fabric by pairing it with a solid-colored backing.

YOU WILL NEED

MATERIALS

- 40in (1m) medium-weight home decor fabric for the pillow front
- 40in (1m) medium-weight home decor fabric for the pillow back
- 20in (50cm) invisible zipper
- Matching thread
- 24 x 24in (60 x 60cm) pillow pad

TOOLS

- Tailor's chalk
- Ruler
- Scissors
- Iron
- Sewing machine
- Zipper foot

Cutting the pieces

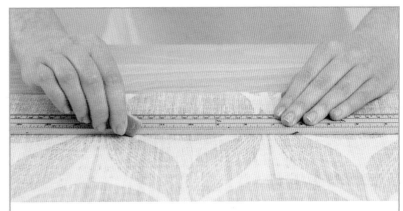

Decide which part of the pattern you would like to show on the front of the pillow. Then, using tailor's chalk and a ruler, measure and mark the exact dimensions of the square pillow pad on the wrong side of the fabric. Cut out the pillow front. Repeat to cut out the pillow back. Neaten all four sides of each square (see p.17).

Inserting the zipper

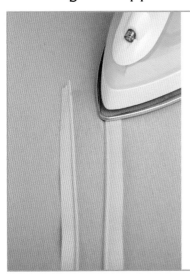

1 To make a neater job of attaching the invisible zipper, lay the open zipper face down on the ironing board. Using the tip of the iron and a synthetic setting, press the zipper tape flat. Avoid leaving the iron on the teeth too long.

2 Along the bottom edge of the pillow front, turn back a ⅝in (1.5cm) seam allowance and press it toward the wrong side of the fabric. Repeat on the pillow back. Turn the front face up and unfold the seam allowance. With the zipper face down and open, center one side of the zipper along the bottom edge, as shown, aligning the teeth with the fold.

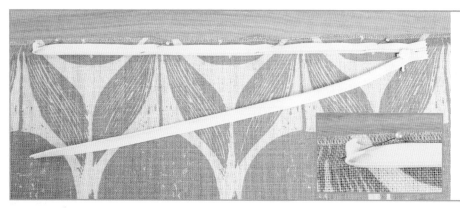

3 Pin the zipper in place along the fold. When you reach the end of the zipper, fold back and pin the excess zipper tape, as shown (inset).

4 Using a zipper foot and adjusting the needle so it is as close to the teeth of the zipper as possible, stitch the zipper in place. Stitch as close to the closed end of the zipper as you can and backstitch at the start and end of the zipper to secure it. Do not sew over the pins but remove them as you go. If you prefer, you can baste the zipper in position, then machine stitch it in place.

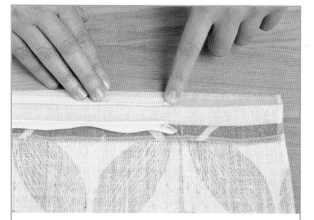

5 With the pillow back right side up, unfold the seam allowance. Place the pillow front on top, right side down. Align the teeth of the unattached side of the zipper with the fold in the pillow back. Check that the front and back of the pillow are aligned, then pin and sew the zipper to the pillow back as before.

Joining front and back

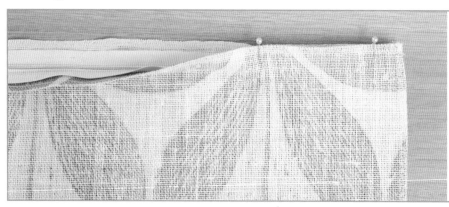

1 With the zipper open and the right sides of the front and back of the pillow cover facing, pin the corners together. Then pin around the edges, placing a pin as close to the beginning and end of the zipper as possible.

2 Using the balance wheel on your sewing machine, lower the needle into the pillow cover at the pin marking the start of the zipper and ⅝in (1.5cm) from the fabric edge. You will be sewing away from the zipper, so make sure the zipper lies behind the presser foot. Check that the needle is as close as possible to the zipper but not on top of the teeth. Backstitch to secure.

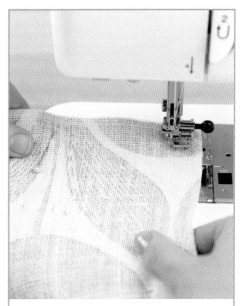

3 Sew to the corner, with a ⅝in (1.5cm) seam allowance. At the corner, with the needle down, lift the presser foot to pivot the fabric. Sew all four sides in the same way until you reach the other end of the zipper.

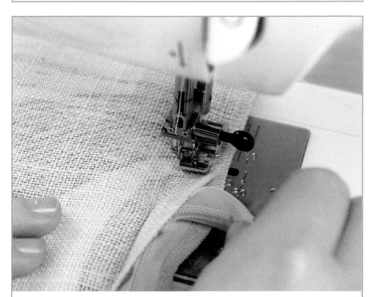

4 As you approach the end of the zipper, remove the pin and pull the end of the zipper toward the seam allowance. Sew as close as possible to the end of the zipper, again using the balance wheel for accuracy. Backstitch to finish.

5 Trim off the corners of the pillow cover to reduce bulk, but make sure you do not cut through your stitches. Turn the cover to the right side and push the corners out. Press to finish and insert a pillow pad.

Oxford pillow

The laid-back luxury of an Oxford pillowcase, its border showcasing a plump pillow, lends relaxed charm to any room in the house and is simplicity itself to sew. The two-part back incorporates a zipper, while the very last step is to stitch the band around the edge.

YOU WILL NEED

MATERIALS
- 18 x 18in (45 x 45cm) pillow pad
- 40in (1m) medium-weight home decor fabric
- Matching thread
- 14in (35cm) invisible zipper

TOOLS
- Tailor's chalk
- Ruler
- Scissors
- Iron
- Pins
- Sewing machine
- Zipper foot
- Masking tape (optional)

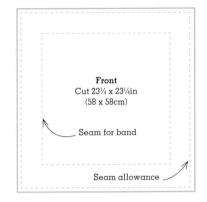

Front
Cut 23¼ x 23¼in
(58 x 58cm)

Seam for band

Seam allowance

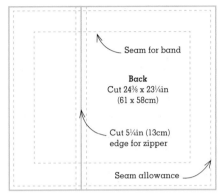

Seam for band

Back
Cut 24⅜ x 23¼in
(61 x 58cm)

Cut 5¼in (13cm)
edge for zipper

Seam allowance

Cutting the front
For the front of a cover to fit an 18in (45cm) pillow pad, cut out a square of fabric 23¼ x 23¼in (58 x 58cm). This allows for the 2in (5cm) wide band all around, plus two ⅝in (1.5cm) seam allowances.

Cutting the back
For the back, cut out a piece of fabric 24⅜ x 23¼in (61 x 58cm). This allows for the 2in (5cm) wide band all around, plus ⅝in (1.5cm) seam allowances, as shown. Cut this piece in two, 5¼in (13cm) from one short edge, to form the opening for the zipper.

Preparing the pieces

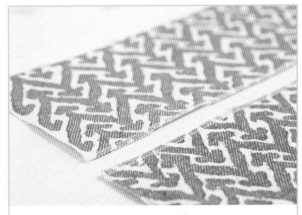

1 Using tailor's chalk and a ruler, measure and mark the dimensions of the front and back of the pillow on the wrong side of the fabric. Cut the pillow back in two, according to the measurements above. Neaten both edges of this cutting line (see p.17).

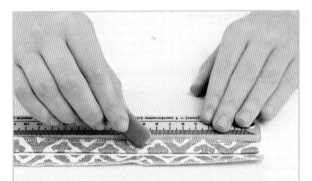

2 With the pillow back pieces face down, fold back then press a ⅝in (1.5cm) seam allowance along the two neatened edges. Mark points 3⅝in (9cm) from each end to indicate where the beginning and end of the zipper will go.

Inserting the zipper

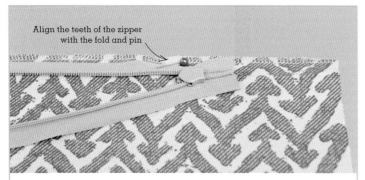

Align the teeth of the zipper
with the fold and pin

1 Unfold the seam allowances. With one of the pillow back pieces right side up and the zipper face down and open, place one side along the neatened edge, aligning the teeth with the fold, ⅝in (1.5cm) from the edge. Pin between the two marks.

2 At the open end of the zipper, fold back and pin the excess tape. Using a zipper foot and with the needle close to the teeth, stitch in place. Sew close to the closed end of the zipper and backstitch at the start and end of the zipper.

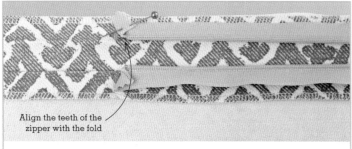

Align the teeth of the
zipper with the fold

3 Lay the other back piece right side up and place the first piece on top, right side down. Align the teeth of the unattached side of the zipper with the other fold. Pin and machine sew the zipper to the other back piece as before.

4 Close the zipper and check that the folded edges of the back pieces are still aligned. If they are not, unpick the zipper, realign it between the marks, and pin it in place, placing a pin every 1¼in (3cm). Stitch in place.

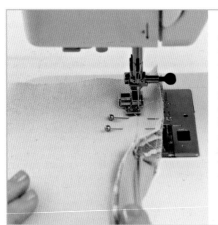

5 With right sides facing, pin the rest of the seam together above and below the zipper. Switch the zipper foot and needle to the left side to allow you to stitch as close as possible to the zipper. Stitch along the pressed fold at both ends of the zipper, sewing as close as possible to the beginning and end of the zipper.

6 Press the seams open from the right side, ensuring that the seam allowance lies flat on each side of the seams.

Joining front and back

1 With the zipper open, place the front and back pieces right sides together. Pin the corners, then pin around the sides. Stitch with a ⅝in (1.5cm) seam allowance around all four sides, pivoting at the corners.

2 Lay the pillow cover flat, with the zipped back piece on top. Press back the seam allowance of the zipped piece all the way around.

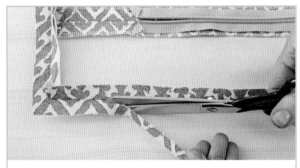

3 Trim the seam allowance of the front piece all the way around. Snip the corners of the back piece. This helps the seam to lie flat when the pillow is turned to the right side.

4 Turn the pillow cover to the right side and push the corners out. Finger-press the edges, rolling the seam toward the edge so that it lies flat. Press.

Creating the band

1 Pin around all four sides of the pillow cover to hold the layers in place, placing the pins perpendicular to the edge.

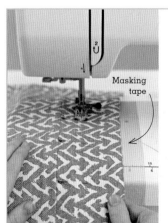

Masking tape

2 Machine stitch 2in (5cm) from the edge, over the pins. Backstitch at the beginning and end. Pivot at the corners. If your needle plate does not have a 2in (5cm) marker, measure this distance to the right of the needle and use a length of masking tape to mark a line. Remove the pins and insert the pillow pad.

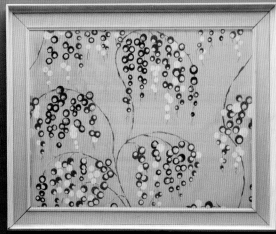

Panel pillow

Contrasting panels of printed and solid-colored fabric in differing widths lend a slightly Asian theme to this rectangular pillow cover. We have made ours in silk, but any fabrics will do, as long as they are all of similar weight. You might even be able to use remnants from your fabric box.

YOU WILL NEED

MATERIALS

- 12 x 20in (30 x 50cm) pillow pad
- 5 or 6 pieces of fabric in various colors and patterns at least 30cm (12in) tall for the pillow front
- 1 piece of fabric large enough to cut a 12 x 20in (30 x 50cm) pillow back
- Matching thread
- 16in (40cm) invisible zipper

TOOLS

- Tailor's chalk
- Scissors
- Pins
- Sewing machine
- Zipper foot
- Ruler

Cutting out the back

Using tailor's chalk and a ruler, measure and mark the exact dimensions of the pillow pad on the wrong side of the pillow back fabric. Cut out the pillow back, then neaten the edges (see p.17).

Making the front

1 Cut the fabrics for the pillow front into pieces that are the height of the pillow pad and approximately one-third of its width.

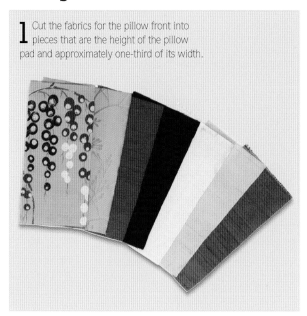

2 Press a ⅝in (1.5cm) seam allowance toward the wrong side of the fabric along the left edge of each piece. Decide the order of the panels and lay them out with right sides facing up. Adjust the overlaps to give some wider and some narrower panels, while checking that the overall width is the same as the pillow back.

3 Once you are happy with the layout, pin one front piece at a time to its adjacent piece, inserting a pin at the top and bottom into the folded seam allowance.

4 Unfold the pressed seam allowance and check that the top and bottom edges of the pieces are level. Add another pin between the top and bottom pins, then baste (see p.18) along the fold line. Remove the pins and trim the excess fabric after tacking (inset).

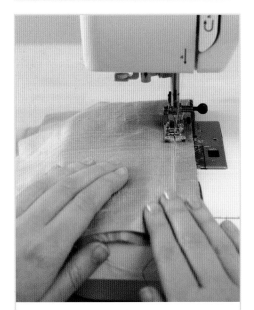

5 Sew the pieces together following the line of basting. Continue pinning, basting, stitching, and trimming the seam allowances until you have joined all the front pieces together. Press each seam open and neaten the edges (see p.17). Finish by pressing the pillow front.

6 Measure the pillow front. If the front is wider than the back, mark with tailor's chalk, then trim.

Inserting the zipper

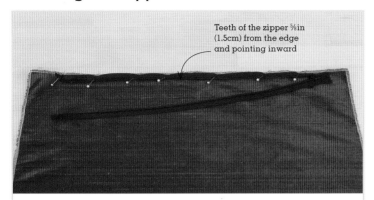

Teeth of the zipper ⅝in (1.5cm) from the edge and pointing inward

1 With the pillow back right side up and the zipper face down and open, center one side of the zipper along one long edge. Position the teeth ⅝in (1.5cm) from the edge. Pin in place. Fold back and pin the excess tape at the end of the zipper. Using a zipper foot and with the needle adjusted so it is as close to the teeth as possible, sew the zipper in place.

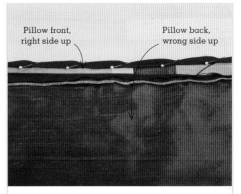

Pillow front, right side up

Pillow back, wrong side up

2 With the pillow front right side up, lay the back with its zipper attached on top. Position the teeth of the other side of the zipper ⅝in (1.5cm) from the edge of the front. Pin and then machine stitch the zipper to the front as before, backstitching at the beginning and end. Open the zipper.

Joining front and back

1 With the right sides of the front and back of the pillow cover facing, pin the corners together, then pin around the edges. Beginning as close as possible to the start of the zipper, backstitch to secure your stitching, then stitch around all four sides with a ⅝in (1.5cm) seam allowance, pivoting at the corners. You can continue with the zipper foot unless your fabric is slippery, in which case change to a straight-stitch foot.

2 When you reach the end of the zipper, pull it toward the seam allowance and then sew as close as possible to the end of the zipper. Backstitch to secure your work. Turn the pillow and insert your pillow pad.

Mitered pillow

Crisp geometry is the focal point of a pillow that is equally at home in the living room or the bedroom. Harnessing the power of stripes and mitered edges, this stylish pillow looks more complex than it is. For a kaleidoscope effect, try the same technique using fabric with an all-over pattern.

YOU WILL NEED

MATERIALS
- 20 x 20in (50 x 50cm) pillow pad
- 40in (1m) light- or medium-weight home decor fabric
- Matching thread
- 16in (40cm) invisible zipper

TOOLS
- Tracing paper
- Scissors
- Pins
- Yardstick
- Pencil
- Sewing machine

Making the pattern and cutting out

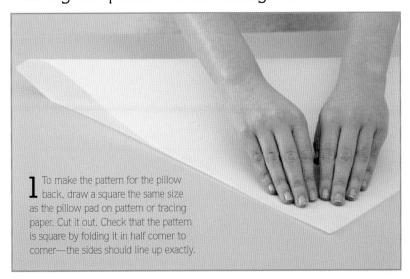

1 To make the pattern for the pillow back, draw a square the same size as the pillow pad on pattern or tracing paper. Cut it out. Check that the pattern is square by folding it in half corner to corner—the sides should line up exactly.

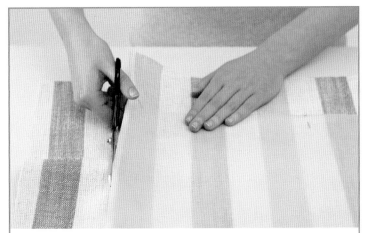

2 Square off the fabric (see p.15), then place the pattern on top. Using tracing paper allows you to see the fabric through the paper. Align the straight edges of the pattern with the stripes on the fabric. Center the pattern, then pin and cut out the pillow back. Neaten the edges of the cut piece (see p.17).

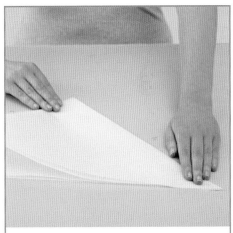

3 To make the pattern for the pillow front, fold the pattern for the back from corner to corner, then fold it in half again. Open it up and cut out one of the triangles.

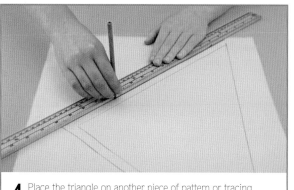

4 Place the triangle on another piece of pattern or tracing paper and trace around it with a pencil. Add a ⅝in (1.5cm) seam allowance to the two sides that form the right angle. Cut out this larger triangle.

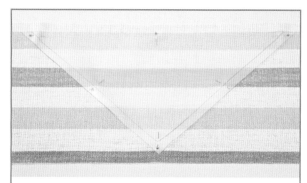

5 Lay the triangular pattern on the fabric and adjust its position to make the most of the striped fabric. Pin the pattern, then cut out the fabric triangle. Cut another three triangles with the stripes in exactly the same place.

Joining the pillow front pieces

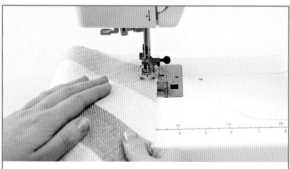

1 Stay stitch (see p.17) along the sides of the fabric triangles, ³⁄₁₆in (8mm) from the edge. Neaten the edges (see p.17). starting from the right-angled point.

2 Matching the stripes. pin two fabric triangles together, right sides facing. along one short side. Machine stitch with a ⅝in (1.5cm) seam allowance. Press the seam open and double-check that the stripes match. Join the other two triangles in the same way.

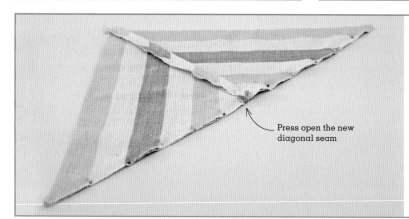

Press open the new diagonal seam

3 Place the joined pieces right sides together. Match the center seams, laying the pressed seam allowances flat against each other. Pin each side of the center seams, then pin the rest of the edge, matching the stripes. Machine stitch together with a ⅝in (1.5cm) seam allowance.

Inserting the zipper

1 With the pillow front right side up and the zipper face down and open, center one side of the zipper along one edge of the pillow front. Position the teeth ⅝in (1.5cm) from the edge. Pin the zipper in place. Fold back and pin the excess tape at the end of the zipper. Using a zipper foot and adjusting the needle so it is as close to the teeth of the zipper as possible, stitch the zipper in place, going as close to its closed end as you can and backstitching at the start and end of the seam to secure your stitching.

Fold back and pin the excess tape

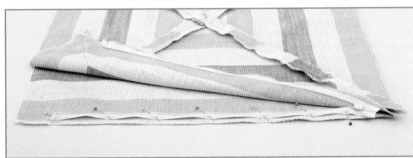

2 With the pillow front on top of the back, right sides together, position the teeth of the other side of the zipper ⅝in (1.5cm) from the edge of the back. Pin and then machine stitch the zipper to the back. Close the zipper, leaving just a hand's width open.

Joining front and back

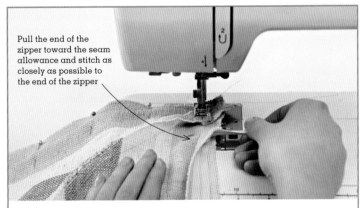

Pull the end of the zipper toward the seam allowance and stitch as closely as possible to the end of the zipper

1 With the pillow front and back right sides together, pin the corners, then the edges. Starting as close to the beginning of the zipper as possible, sew with a ⅝in (1.5cm) seam allowance around all four sides, pivoting at the corners. When you reach the end of the zipper, pull it toward the seam allowance, then sew as closely as possible to the end of the zipper. Backstitch to secure.

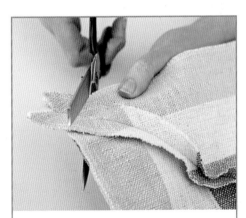

2 Clip the corners to reduce bulk, but do not cut through your stitches. Turn the cover to the right side, push out the corners, then press and insert the pillow pad.

Tuck-front pillow

Tucks in different widths and of varying complexity are a great way to enliven an otherwise plain pillow. Here a single tuck and a double tuck combine to bring an air of quiet elegance to a comfy plump pillow.

YOU WILL NEED

MATERIALS

- Medium-weight home decor fabric
- Matching thread
- Contrasting thread
- 12in (30cm) invisible zipper
- 16 x 16in (40 x 40cm) pillow pad

TOOLS

- Scissors
- Ruler
- Tailor's chalk in two colors
- Hand sewing needle
- Pins
- Sewing machine
- Masking tape (optional)
- Iron
- Zipper foot

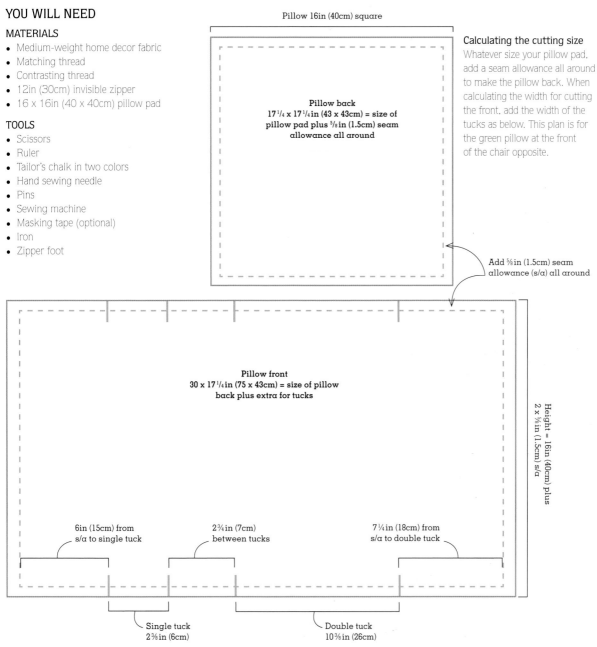

Pillow 16in (40cm) square

Pillow back
17¼ x 17¼ in (43 x 43cm) = size of
pillow pad plus ⅝ in (1.5cm) seam
allowance all around

Calculating the cutting size
Whatever size your pillow pad, add a seam allowance all around to make the pillow back. When calculating the width for cutting the front, add the width of the tucks as below. This plan is for the green pillow at the front of the chair opposite.

Add ⅝ in (1.5cm) seam
allowance (s/a) all around

Pillow front
30 x 17¼ in (75 x 43cm) = size of pillow
back plus extra for tucks

Height = 16in (40cm) plus
2 x ⅝ in (1.5cm) s/a

6in (15cm) from
s/a to single tuck

2¾ in (7cm)
between tucks

7¼ in (18cm) from
s/a to double tuck

Single tuck
2⅜ in (6cm)

Double tuck
10⅜ in (26cm)

Cutting out and marking

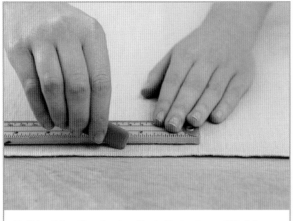

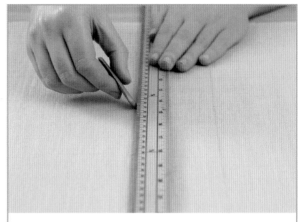

1 Cut out the pillow front and back. Neaten (see p.17) all the edges. Lay the front face down. Using tailor's chalk and a ruler, transfer all the tuck markings to the fabric along the top and bottom edges (see diagram on preceding page).

2 Join the marks from top to bottom. The pair of lines that are 2⅜in (6cm) apart mark the single tuck. The set of lines that are 10⅜in (26cm) apart mark the double tuck.

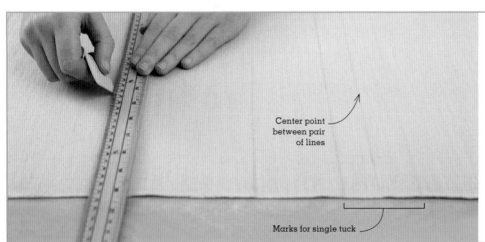

Center point
between pair
of lines

Marks for single tuck

3 Using a ruler and a different colored chalk, measure and mark a line centrally between each pair of tuck lines.

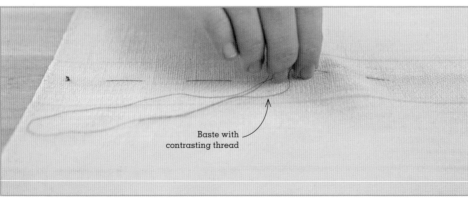

Baste with
contrasting thread

4 Baste (see p.18) along the center line of each tuck.

Creating the tucks

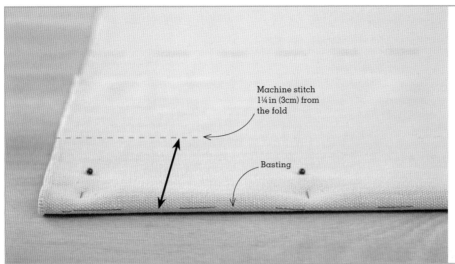

Machine stitch 1¼in (3cm) from the fold

Basting

1 Fold the fabric with wrong sides facing along the line of basting between the 2⅜in (6cm) lines to make a single tuck. Ensure that the top and bottom edges of the fabric are aligned. Secure with pins. Machine stitch from top to bottom, 1¼in (3cm) from the fold and over the chalk line. If your needle plate does not have a 1¼in (3cm) marker, measure this distance to the right of the needle and use a length of masking tape to mark a line.

2 Open out the fabric. With wrong sides facing, fold along the line of basting between the 10⅜in (26cm) lines to make the double tuck, ensuring the edges are aligned. Pin in place.

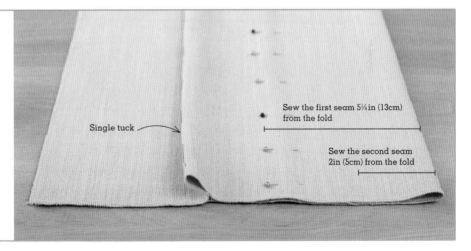

Single tuck

Sew the first seam 5¼in (13cm) from the fold

Sew the second seam 2in (5cm) from the fold

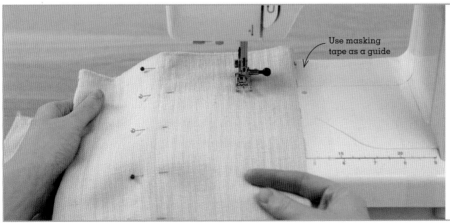

Use masking tape as a guide

3 Machine stitch from top to bottom 5¼in (13cm) from the folded edge. To help keep your stitching straight, measure 5¼in (13cm) to the right of the needle and use a length of masking tape to mark a line. Stitch a second seam 2in (5cm) from the folded edge. Again, use a length of masking tape to help keep the stitching straight.

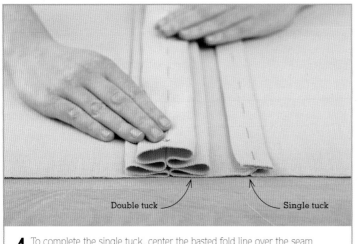

Double tuck — � — Single tuck

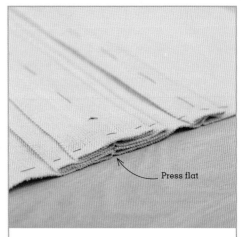

Press flat ⏤

4 To complete the single tuck, center the basted fold line over the seam made in Step 1. Press in place. For the double tuck, center the basted fold line first over the 2in (5cm) seam and then over the 5¼in (13cm) seam made in Step 3. Press in place.

5 Secure the ends of the tucks with pins then baste in place. Press.

Inserting the zipper

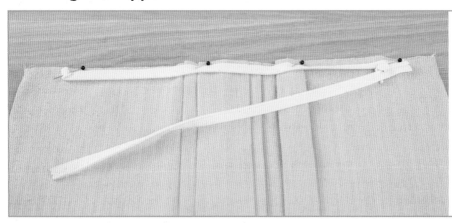

1 With the pillow front right side up and the zipper face down and open, center the zipper across the folds at one edge with the teeth of the zipper ⅝in (1.5cm) from the edge. Pin in place, folding back and pinning the excess tape at the open end of the zipper. Sew the zipper in place using a zipper foot, stitching as close to the teeth of the zipper as possible.

2 Lay the pillow front on top of the back, right sides together. Pin the other side of the zipper along the edge of the back and stitch in place. Close the zipper, leaving just a hand's width open.

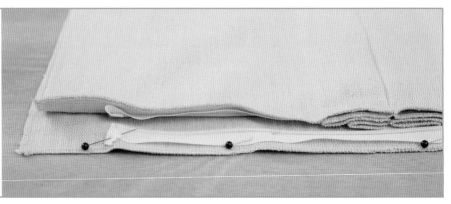

Joining front and back

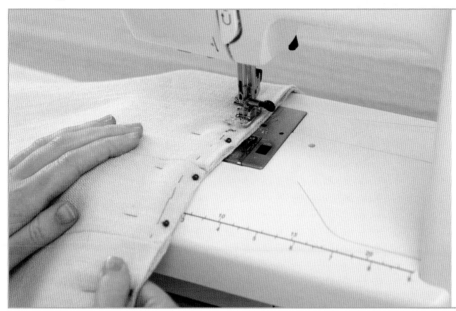

1 With the right sides of the pillow front and back facing, pin the corners together. Then pin around the edges. Starting at the end of the zipper and with a ⅝in (1.5cm) seam allowance, machine stitch around the pillow to the other end of the zipper, pivoting at the corners. Stitch as close to the ends of the zipper as possible.

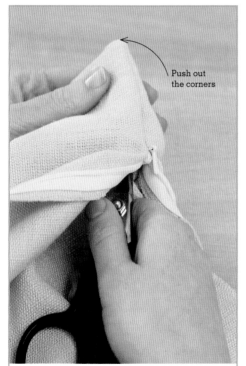

Push out the corners

2 Remove the basting stitches. Clip the corners to reduce bulk, but do not cut through your stitches.

3 Turn the cover to the right side, push out the corners, then press and insert the pillow pad.

Bean bag

Sassy stripes give a modern twist to a comfortable, squashy bean bag chair that is equally at home in a living room as in a child's bedroom. With its neat, sturdy handle, this spare chair can be carried to wherever you happen to need extra seating. As a bonus, the zipped cover can be easily removed for cleaning.

YOU WILL NEED

MATERIALS

- 120in (3m) light- or medium-weight home decor fabric
- Zipper 28in (70cm)
- 120in (3m) muslin or cotton batiste for lining bag
- 2 x 1lb (450g) bags of polystyrene fire-retardant beads for filling
- Matching thread

TOOLS

- Paper or muslin for pattern
- Photocopier
- Pencil
- Fabric marker
- Pins
- Scissors
- Sewing machine
- Zipper foot
- Large posterboard to use as a funnel

Bean bag construction
The bean bag is made up of five equally sized sections. The handle is attached to a five-sided panel stitched to the top.

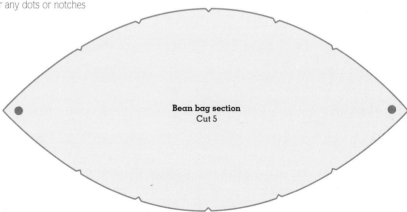

MAKING THE PATTERN PIECES

Turn to pp.208–209 for the templates for the bean bag pieces. Photocopy or trace the template for the top and cut it out. Enlarge the bean bag section on the photocopier. Cut out the enlarged pieces and tape them together. You may choose to trace around the taped piece onto muslin or pattern paper to make a more versatile pattern piece. Don't forget to transfer any dots or notches to your pattern piece.

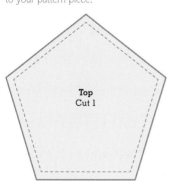

Preparing the bean bag sections

1 Lay the pattern on your main fabric to make the most of the fabric's design. Here we align the point of the pattern with the middle of a stripe. Pin, then cut out. Repeat to make five bean bag sections, then repeat to make five lining pieces.

2 Transfer the notch and dot markings from the template to each bean bag section.

3 Stay stitch (see p.17) ⅜in (1cm) from the edge between the first and last notches on each fabric piece to prevent the fabric from stretching along the curve. Neaten the edges (see p.17).

Making the handle

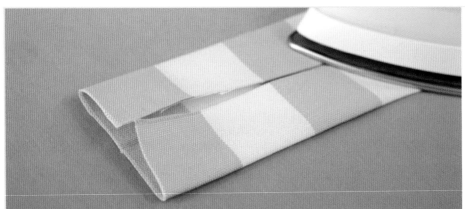

1 Cut out a rectangle 12⅜in (31cm) long and 6⅜in (16cm) wide for the handle. Fold in half lengthwise, wrong sides facing, then press. Open it out, then fold the raw edges into the center fold and press again.

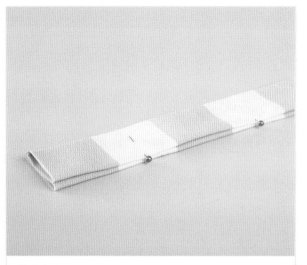

2 Refold along the center line, matching the folded edges. Secure with pins.

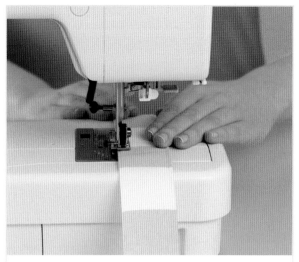

3 Using a medium-length stitch, topstitch (see p.16) along each long side of the strip as close to the edge as possible. Press again to set the stitches.

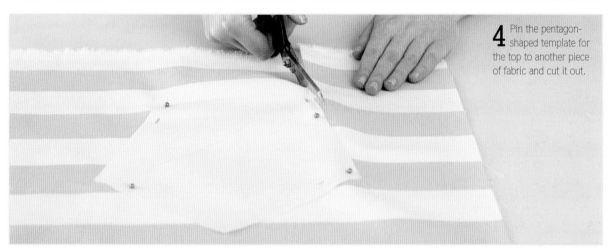

4 Pin the pentagon-shaped template for the top to another piece of fabric and cut it out.

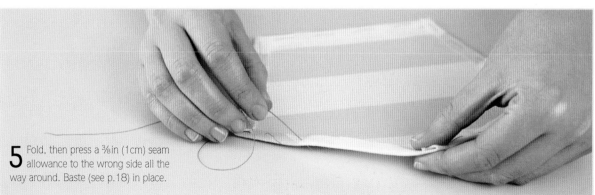

5 Fold, then press a ⅜in (1cm) seam allowance to the wrong side all the way around. Baste (see p.18) in place.

Inserting the zipper

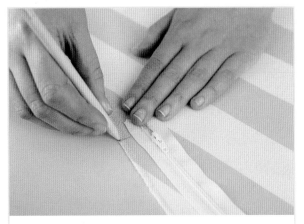

1 Lay one bean bag section right side up. Center the zipper in the middle of one curved side. Mark the fabric at the beginning and end of the zipper.

2 Lay another section on top, right sides together and matching the notches. Transfer the zipper markings to the right side of the second section. Fold under, then press a ⅝in (1.5cm) seam allowance between the notches.

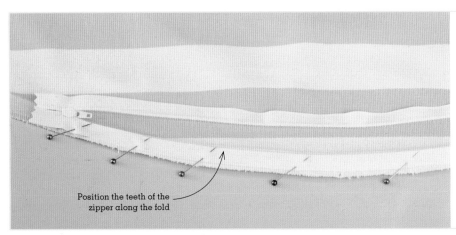

Position the teeth of the zipper along the fold

3 With the fabric right side up and the zipper face down and open, place one side of the zipper along the edge, between the zipper markings, with the teeth aligned with the fold. Fold back and pin the excess zipper tape, then pin and stitch the zipper in place using a zipper foot. Stitch as close to the teeth of the zipper as possible.

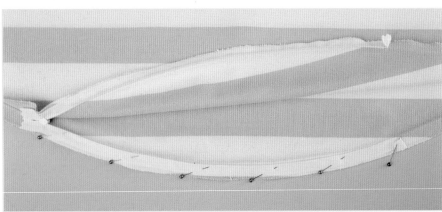

4 Lay the zipped section on top of the other section, right sides together. Align the teeth of the unattached side of the zipper with the fold in the second section. Fold back and pin the excess zipper tape, then pin and stitch the zipper in place as before.

5 With the zipper open, lay the two sections, right sides together with notches matching. Pin together along the seam allowance, starting from the marked dot and finishing at the zipper. Repeat at the other end of the zipper.

6 Stitch along each pinned edge with a ⅝in (1.5cm) seam allowance, starting at the dot at each end. When you reach the end of the zipper, pull the end of the zipper toward the seam allowance, then sew as close as possible to the end of the zipper. Press the seam allowance open.

Joining the sections

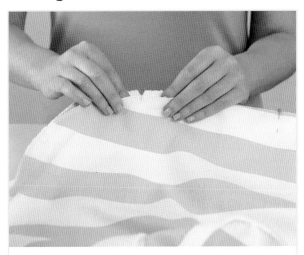

1 With right sides together and notches matching, lay the edge of a third section along the free edge of the second section. Pin at the notches along the whole edge.

2 Check that the sections are aligned at the top and bottom. Pin and stitch, starting and ending at the dots. Make sure that you are only stitching through two sections at a time and that any other fabric is held out of the way. Continue joining the sections in the same way, until you have joined all five.

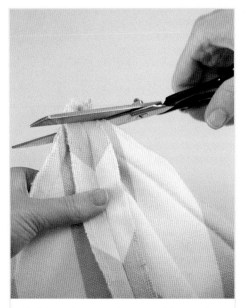

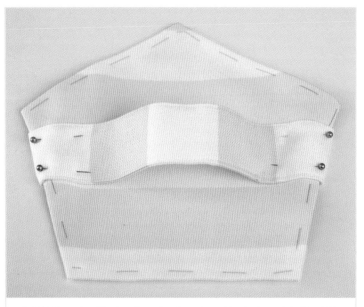

3 Trim off the seam allowances at the point to reduce bulk, but make sure you do not cut through your stitches.

4 Fold the ends of the handle under, then pin and baste the ends to the right side of the fabric pentagon, as shown. Leave some slack in the handle so there is room to hold it.

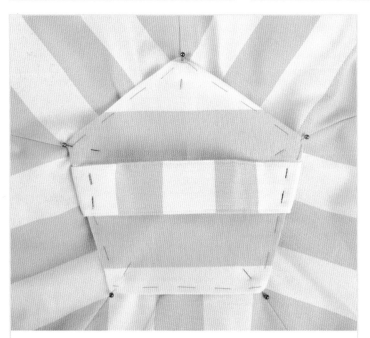

5 Turn the bean bag to the right side and lay it out so that the point where all five sections meet is lying as flat as possible. This can be tricky, because you are trying to lay a spherical shape flat. Place the pentagon on top, right side up and matching its points to the five seams. Pin at each point.

6 Pin the pentagon to the bean bag along all five sides, easing the fabric of the bean bag so it fits between the five pinned points.

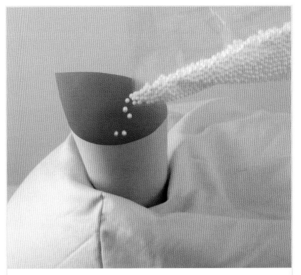

7 Using a number 3 stitch, topstitch the pentagon in place, as close to the edges as possible and pivoting at the points. Make sure that the fabric does not bunch up underneath the needle and that the seam allowances on the wrong side of the bean bag lie flat.

8 Make a lining bag using the lining pieces and joining them as in Steps 1–3. When you join the last section to the previous one, leave a gap between the 2nd and 4th notches. Make a wide funnel from a piece of stiff posterboard, insert it in the gap, and use it to fill the bag with polystyrene beads.

9 Topstitch the opening closed. Place the filled lining bag inside the bean bag cover and close the zipper.

Pillow trims

Whether the pillow covers you make are bright or muted, patterned or solid-colored, a great way to give them some extra pizzazz, personality, and a professional finish is to add a decorative trim. You can easily make a piping trim from matching or contrasting fabric, or you can buy beaded trims, pom-pom trims, and other novelty trims ready-made.

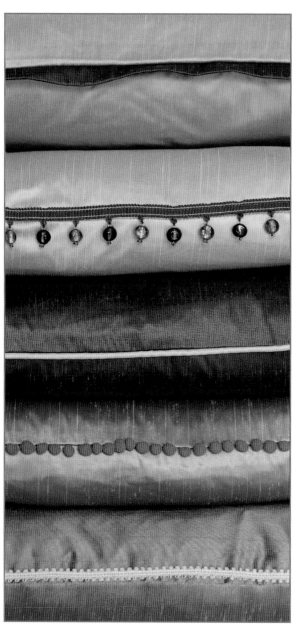

Flat piping

Flat piping is made in a similar way to regular piping, but is less tricky because it doesn't need to be cut on the bias. Nor does it involve sewing piping cord inside. As with regular piping, the raw edges are hidden in the seam as the piping is sewn in place. The finished piping adds a sophisticated look to your pillow.

Beading

There's no need to worry about sewing individual beads on a ribbon with this trim, since you can buy it ready-made online or in fabric stores. You can sew the beaded trim into the seam of your pillow as you join the pillow pieces together: that way the beads appear to be coming out of the seam. Alternatively, as here, you can slip stitch the trim around the edge of your pillow.

Piping

Piping is created by stitching piping cord into a length of either matching or contrasting fabric that has been cut on the bias (see pp.59–61). Once you've completed that step, you join the pillow pieces together, enclosing the raw edges of the piping in the seam. This popular trim will give your pillow a neat, tailored look.

Pom-poms

Pom-pom trim consists of pom-poms attached to a ribbon—much like beading trim—and, as with piping, you usually sew the ribbon part into the seam as you join your pillow pieces together. Pom-poms come in all colors and sizes, and will give your pillow a fun, quirky finish. When you turn the pillow to the right side to press the seam, make sure that you don't squash the pom-poms with your iron.

Ribbon

The sky's the limit when it comes to the myriad colors, widths, weaves, and finishes of the ribbons that are on the market. You can really go to town with ribbon, using it to add a truly personal touch to your pillows. Either machine stitch it to the pillow cover before you join the pillow pieces together, or hand stitch it in place afterward.

Making piping

Piping, whether in matching or contrasting fabric, gives a smart and tailored finish to pillows and slipcovers and is easy to make. Strips are cut on the bias and joined. Piping cord is then stitched in.

Cutting the bias strips

1 Place the fabric on the work surface wrong side up. Find the bias (see p.14) by folding the top corner to the bottom edge so that the edges are aligned. Press the diagonal fold. This is the bias.

2 Open out the fabric and cut along the fold.

3 Measure and mark 1 ⅝in (4cm) at regular intervals along the cut edge.

4 Join the marks together with a line. Mark more lines with the same spacing between them as many times as necessary until you have the number of strips required. Cut along the lines to cut the bias strips.

Joining the strips

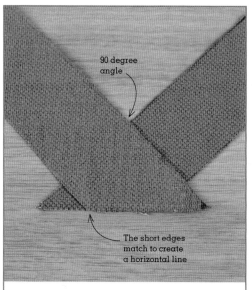

90 degree angle

The short edges match to create a horizontal line

1 Lay two strips right side to right side at 90 degrees to each other, matching their short edges to make a horizontal line. Move the top strip so that its outer corner sits 1 in (2.5cm) in from the outer corner of the bottom strip.

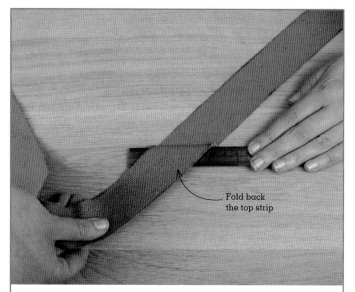

Fold back the top strip

2 Place a ruler over the aligned short edges to hold the strips together at the horizontal line, then fold back the top strip over the ruler. If the line formed by the long edges of the strips looks continuous, then the strips are in the correct position. Adjust them if they they are uneven.

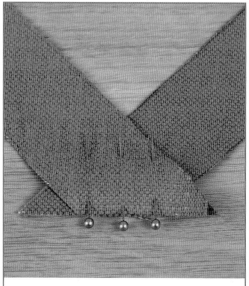

3 Fold the top strip back and secure the short edges with vertical pins across the horizontal line.

4 Place the strips under the foot so that the horizontal line is parallel to the lines on the needle plate grid (see p.8). Machine stitch across the pins with a ⅝in (1.5cm) seam allowance. Repeat, joining more strips until you have the length required.

5 Press the seams open and trim off the corners at each seam.

Sewing the piping

1 Square off one end of the completed bias strip. Measure and cut the strip to the required length and square off the other end. Be careful not to stretch the strip when measuring.

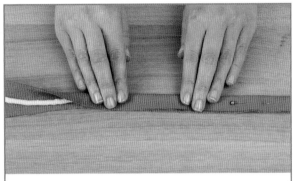

2 Cut piping cord to the length of the strip. With the bias strip face down, lay the piping cord along the middle of the strip. Fold the strip over the cord, keeping the cord centered and matching the raw edges of the fabric. Secure with pins, leaving the first 3 ¼in (8cm) of the strip unpinned.

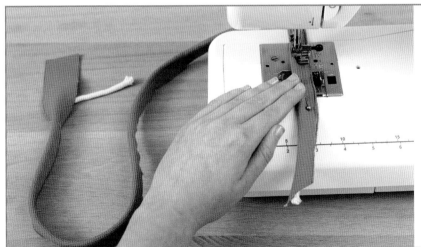

3 Using a piping or zipper foot, place the strip under the foot and lower the needle at the start of the pins. Ensuring that the piping cord is under the notch in the foot, machine stitch in place, making sure that the raw edges of the strip stay aligned. Do not backstitch at the start or finish. Leave about 3 ¼in (8cm) unstitched at the end.

Round pillow

Contrast piping and a button lend a touch of glamour to a round pillow that would grace any sofa, chair, or bed. The design of this fixed cover works equally well in a patterned fabric; simply pick out one of the colors for the piping.

YOU WILL NEED

MATERIALS
- Muslin
- Medium-weight fabric in main color
- Matching thread
- Piping cord
- Light- or medium-weight fabric in contrasting color for piping and buttons
- Contrasting thread
- Round pillow pad
- Two metal self-cover buttons
- Nylon twine

TOOLS
- Ruler
- Pencil
- Masking tape
- Compass or string
- Scissors
- Pins
- Hand sewing needle
- Sewing machine
- Zipper foot
- Pliers (optional)
- Upholstery needle

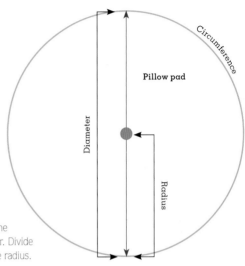

Measuring
Measure the distance across the pillow pad to find the diameter. Divide this amount by two to find the radius.

Making the pattern and cutting out

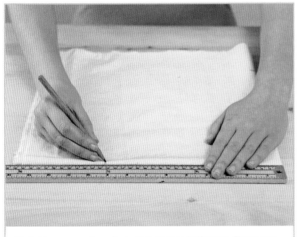

1 Fold a square of muslin in half, then in half again. Figure out the radius of the pillow pad, then add a ⅝in (1.5cm) seam allowance. Measure and mark this distance on two adjacent edges of the muslin, starting at the folded center point.

2 Tape the folded muslin to the work surface. Use a compass to draw an arc from mark to mark or tie a pencil to a piece of string. Hold the pencil at one of the marks and, holding the string taut, pin the other end of the string to the folded center point. Hold the pencil upright at one mark and draw the arc to the second mark. Cut along the arc to cut out the pattern piece. Open up.

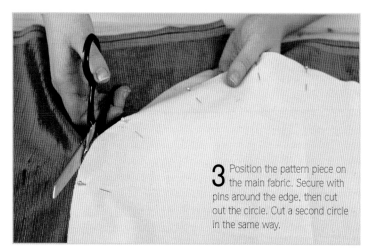

3 Position the pattern piece on the main fabric. Secure with pins around the edge, then cut out the circle. Cut a second circle in the same way.

4 Fold each fabric circle in half, then in half again. Make a single basting stitch through the center point of each fabric circle.

5 Open out the circle and make a few more basting stitches. The basting stitches mark where the button will be attached later.

Attaching the piping

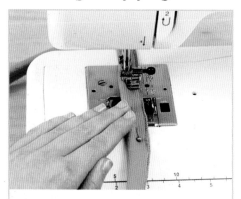

1 Make piping (see pp.59–61) from the contrasting fabric, at least 1⅝in (4cm) longer than the circumference of the fabric circle.

2 Cut notches into the seam allowance of the piping. Align the raw edge of the piping with the edge of one fabric circle and pin in place. Leaving 4in (10cm) of piping unstitched at each end, machine the piping to the fabric. Use a zipper foot positioned next to the stitching on the piping.

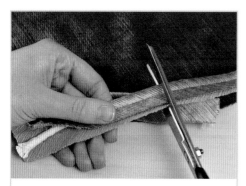

3 Lay the cut ends of the piping on top of each other, then cut the piping casing to give a 1⅝in (4cm) overlap.

4 Open out each end of the piping casing, pull the piping cord out of the way, and hold the ends with the wrong side of each facing you. Leaving the left-hand end where it is, twist the right-hand end away from you so the right side of the casing is now facing you.

5 Holding the ends in this position, overlap them, left over right, so that the short end of the left-hand piece lines up with the long edge of the right-hand piece, and the corners match up. Pin from top to bottom, as shown.

Stitch line

6 Machine stitch the two ends together across the corner over the pins. Remove the pins and trim the raw edges of the seam to ⅜in (1cm).

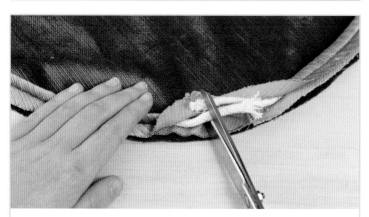

7 With the casing opened out, overlap the ends of the piping cord and cut them level. Do not cut directly on top of the seam in the casing, since this will lead to too much bulk.

8 Tuck the ends of the cord inside the casing, then bring the raw edges of the casing together. Pin, then machine stitch them closed.

Joining the front and back

1 Stay stitch (see p.17) the other fabric circle within the seam allowance. This is the pillow back. Fold in half, then in half again and mark the half and quarter points with pins. Repeat on the pillow front.

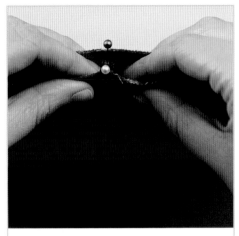

2 With right sides together and matching the half and quarter points, pin the front and back together. Ease in any excess fabric.

3 With the circle that has the piping attached on top, and using a zipper foot, machine between three of the markers, leaving an opening. Having the piping on top helps you ease in the excess fabric as you sew.

4 Turn the pillow cover to the right side and insert the pillow pad. Pin the opening closed, starting from the middle of the opening and working toward either end.

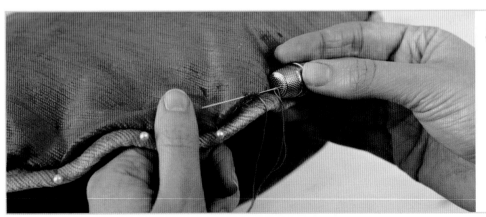

5 Slip stitch the opening closed.

Covering the buttons

1 Cut a circle from the contrasting fabric approximately ¾in (2cm) bigger all around than the button to be covered. Holding the button and fabric circle together, snip notches around the edge of the fabric to ease it around the curve.

2 Hold the button and fabric together in one hand and use the other hand to push the fabric over the edge of the button until the fabric catches on the teeth.

Snip off any excess fabric as you go

3 Continue until the fabric is caught on the teeth all the way around. As you go, check that the fabric is taut on the front of the button and snip off any excess fabric. This is tricky and takes time and patience. Don't snip too close to the teeth or the fabric will fray.

4 Snap the back of the button in place, using pliers if necessary. Repeat to cover a second button.

Attaching the buttons

1 Feed a long piece of nylon twine through the shank of one of the buttons, then thread the free ends of the twine through the eye of the upholstery needle.

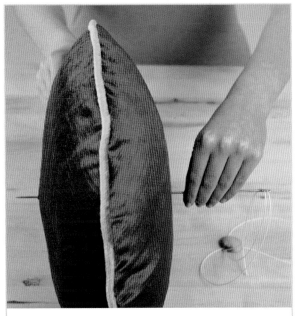

2 Push the needle straight through the pillow at one marked center point and out through the second center point on the other side. Keep the needle as straight as possible all the time.

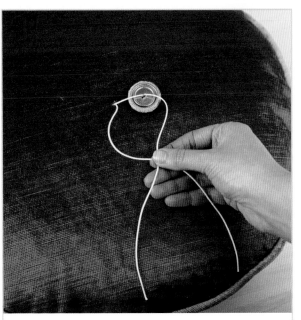

3 Remove the needle, then thread one free end of the twine through the shank of the second button. Pinch the two ends of twine between your thumb and index finger.

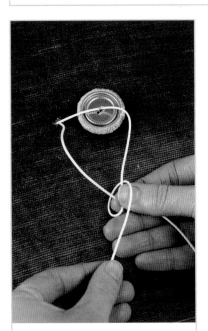

4 Loop the left-hand end of the twine under and then over the right-hand end.

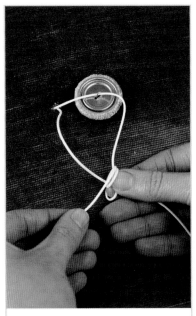

5 Loop it under and over the right-hand end a second time to form a slip knot.

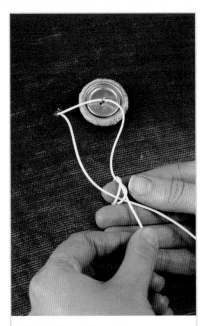

6 Pull the end through the original loop.

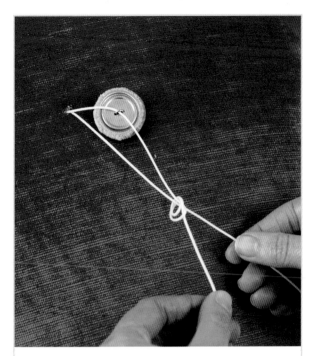

7 Pull the right-hand piece of twine until the knot tightens.

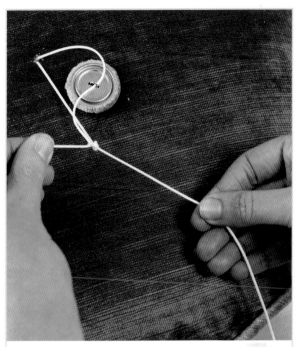

8 Pull on the right-hand piece so the knot moves toward the button.

9 Pull hard to make the knot as tight as possible.

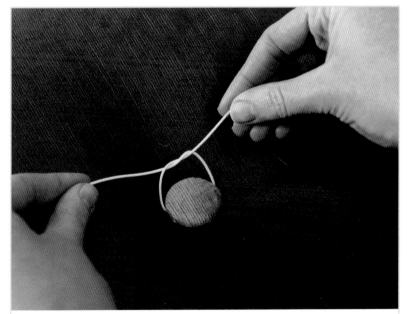

10 Once the buttons fit snugly in the pillow, wrap the remaining twine around the button once and tie a couple of knots to secure. Snip off the ends of the twine.

Bolster pillow

Emphasizing the cylindrical shape of the bolster, the candy-colored stripes and contrasting end pieces of this bolster cover are sure to add a wow factor to a neutral sofa or bed. Matching piping around the ends gives a neatly tailored look, and the whole cover unzips for easy removal. If stripes aren't for you, try a patterned fabric with contrast piping and ends, or use two boldly contrasting solids.

YOU WILL NEED

MATERIALS
- Main fabric plus extra for piping
- Contrasting fabric for ends
- Matching thread
- Piping cord
- Invisible zipper. 2in (5cm) shorter than the pillow pad length
- Bolster pad

TOOLS
- Sewing machine
- Zipper foot
- Compass
- Pencil
- Ruler
- Pins
- Yardstick (or measuring tape)
- Scissors
- Tracing paper

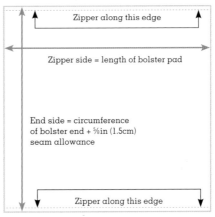

Bolster body

Zipper along this edge

Zipper side = length of bolster pad

End side = circumference of bolster end + ⅝in (1.5cm) seam allowance

Zipper along this edge

CUTTING MEASUREMENTS
Measure the diameter and length of the bolster pad and then figure out the measurements as below.

Diameter — Length

Bolster end

Diameter + seam allowance

Calculating the circumference
To find the circumference of the bolster end (also the length of the end side of the bolster body) multiply the diameter of the bolster pad by π (3.14).

Cutting the pattern

1 For the ends of the bolster, divide the diameter of the bolster pad by two. Set your compass to this measurement and draw a circle on paper. Now add ⅝in (1.5cm) to your compass setting and draw a second circle outside the first. Cut out the pattern piece around the second circle.

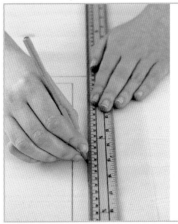

2 For the bolster body, figure out the measurements from the diagram (see above). Draw this rectangle on paper, then add a ⅝in (1.5cm) seam allowance to the end side measurement (see diagram). The zipper sides and end sides may look similar in length so label them on the pattern.

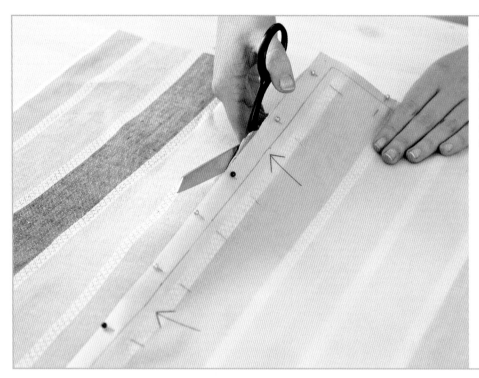

3 If using striped fabric, place the pattern for the bolster body so that the end side is parallel to the stripes. Cut out, then neaten (see p.17) the zipper edges. Pin the pattern for the ends to the contrasting fabric and cut two end pieces.

Inserting the zipper

Start stitching 2in (5cm) from the closed end of the zipper (marked here with a pin)

Position the open end of the zipper 2in (5cm) in from the edge

1 With the bolster body right side up and the zipper face down and open, place one side of the zipper with its teeth ⅝in (1.5cm) from the neatened edge and with its open end 2in (5cm) from the raw edge. Pin in place, folding back and pinning the excess tape at the end of the zipper. Starting 2in (5cm) from the closed end, stitch the zipper in place, stitching as close to the teeth of the zipper as possible.

Start stitching 2in (5cm) from
the closed end of the zipper

2 Turn the body around so the other neatened edge is facing you. Pick up the edge with the zipper and match the second side of the zipper to the other neatened edge. Pin the zipper in place with the teeth ⅝in (1.5cm) from the edge. If using striped fabric, put a pin on every stripe to make sure the stripes match. Stitch in place, again starting 2in (5cm) from the closed edge of the zipper.

3 Pin the open ends of the zipper side together. Stitch to the marker pins, pulling the end of the zipper out of the way to sew as closely as possible to the zipper.

4 Topstitch four or five stitches across each end of the zipper and backstitch at the start and end to strengthen.

Making the ends of the bolster

1 Stay stitch ⅜in (1cm) from the edge of the end pieces (see p.17) to help to stabilize the circles.

Snip the seam allowance at ⅝in (1.5cm) intervals to ease the piping around the curves

2 Make two lengths of piping (see pp.59–61) from the main fabric, at least 1⅝in (4cm) longer than the circumference of the bolster. Leave 2in (5cm) of each end unstitched.

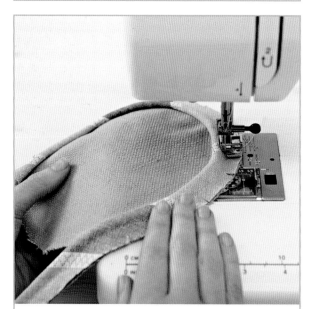

3 Align the raw edge of the piping with the edge of an end piece. Using a zipper foot, machine stitch the piping to the end piece, leaving 2in (5cm) unstitched at the start and finish.

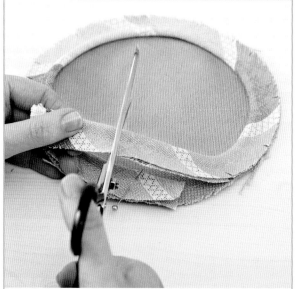

4 Lay the end piece right side up, with the unstitched ends lying on top of each other. Measure and mark the casing to give an overlap of 1⅝in (4cm). Trim the excess.

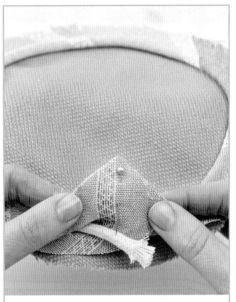

5 Pull the piping cord out of the way. Open out each end of the piping casing and hold the ends with the wrong side of each facing you. Leaving the left-hand end where it is, twist the right-hand end away from you so the right side of the casing is now facing you.

6 Holding the ends in this position, overlap them, left over right, so that the short end of the left-hand piece lines up with the long edge of the right-hand piece, and the corners match up. Pin from top to bottom, as shown.

7 Machine stitch the two ends together, across the pin. Remove the pin and trim the seam allowance to ⅜in (1cm).

8 With the casing opened out, overlap the ends of the piping cord and cut them level. Do not cut directly on top of the seam in the casing, since this leads to too much bulk. Tuck the ends of the cord inside the casing.

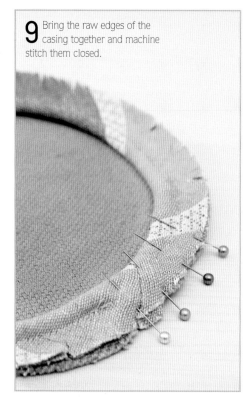

9 Bring the raw edges of the casing together and machine stitch them closed.

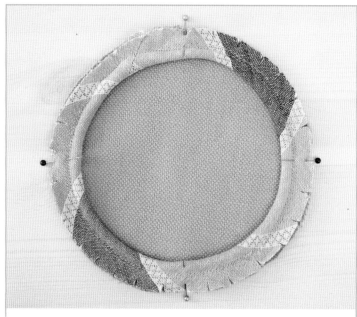

10 Fold the end piece in half and mark the halfway point with pins on opposite edges. Fold in half again the other way and mark the quarter points. Avoid folding directly on the seam in the casing. Repeat Steps 3–10 for the other end piece.

Joining the body and the ends

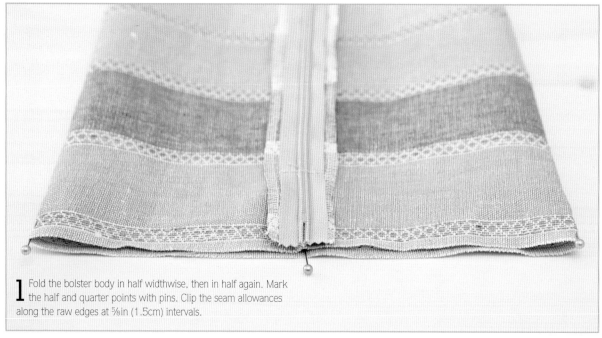

1 Fold the bolster body in half widthwise, then in half again. Mark the half and quarter points with pins. Clip the seam allowances along the raw edges at ⅝in (1.5cm) intervals.

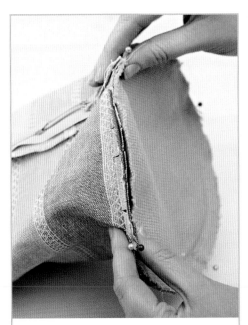

2 With right sides together, first match the half and quarter pins on the body and on one end piece, then pin all the way around, matching the raw edges.

3 Using the zipper foot and with the bolster body on top, stitch the two pieces together. Stitch as close to the piping as possible and pull gently on the body so that all the raw edges are aligned. Turn to the right side to check the stitching. If the stitches are visible alongside the piping or if the piping feels too loose, stitch around again, this time a little closer to the piping. Open the zipper, then repeat Steps 2 and 3 to attach the other end piece to the body.

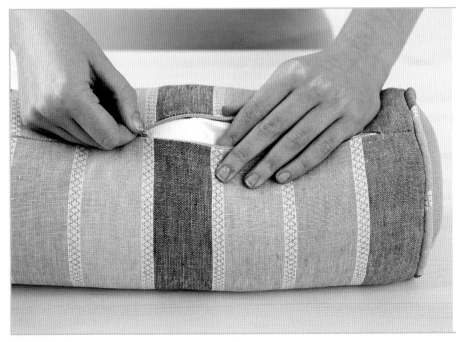

4 Place the bolster pad inside the cover. It should be a tight fit. Manipulate the cover so that the bolster pad fits inside evenly. Close the zipper.

Piped seat pad

Contrasting piping never dates, nor do zingy, classic cotton prints. Here the two combine to make a piped seat cushion cover for a boldly colored, modern, plastic chair that works indoors as well as out. The seat cushion is attached to the chair with fabric ties and the entire cover easily unzips for washing.

YOU WILL NEED

MATERIALS
- Main fabric
- Contrasting fabric for piping
- Muslin for pattern
- Invisible zipper
- Matching thread
- Piping cord
- Foam pad of 2in (5cm) thickness

TOOLS
- Scissors
- Masking tape (optional)
- Tailor's chalk
- Sewing gauge
- Sewing machine
- Zipper foot
- Tape measure
- Iron

Cutting the foam pad to shape
Use the muslin fabric pattern you make as part of this project to cut your foam pad. Just trim off the seam allowance, draw around the pattern piece and cut out along the line.

Making the pattern

1 Drape the muslin over the chair seat, then smooth it out and over the edges. Secure with a little masking tape if necessary. Use tailor's chalk to mark the perimeter of the seat accurately on the fabric.

2 Mark the position of the two uprights (the chair stiles) with a line on the fabric on each side. This is where the ties will be attached.

3 Remove the pattern and fold it in half to check that it is symmetrical. Adjust if necessary.

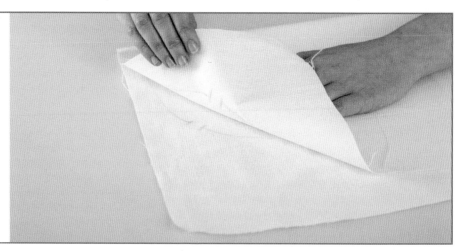

4 Lay the pattern flat on the work surface and use a sewing gauge and tailor's chalk to mark a series of points ¾ in (2cm) from the seat perimeter. Join the points. This will be your cutting line. It allows for a ⅝ in (1.5cm) seam allowance and ³⁄₁₆ in (5mm) for ease, so the fabric can be wrapped around the seat cushion. Cut out the pattern.

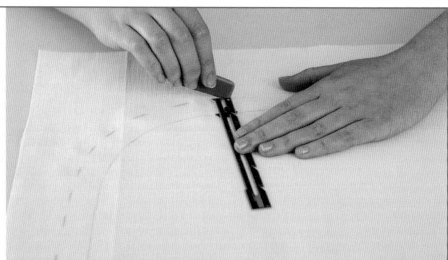

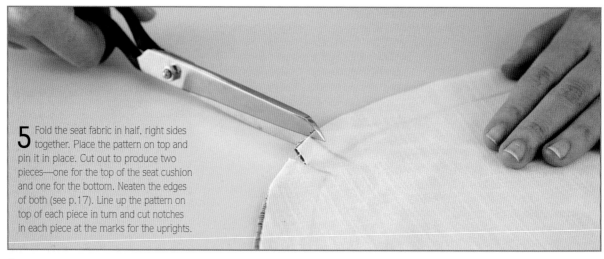

5 Fold the seat fabric in half, right sides together. Place the pattern on top and pin it in place. Cut out to produce two pieces—one for the top of the seat cushion and one for the bottom. Neaten the edges of both (see p.17). Line up the pattern on top of each piece in turn and cut notches in each piece at the marks for the uprights.

Attaching the piping

1 Put a pin in the edge of one piece of seat fabric and from here measure the perimeter. Make a length of piping (see pp.59–61) at least 1⅝in (4cm) longer than the perimeter.

2 Starting at the back of the seat and leaving 3in (8cm) of piping unattached at the start, pin the piping to one of the seat pieces. Align the raw edge of the piping with the neatened edge of the seat fabric. To ease the piping around the curves, cut a few notches into its seam allowance. Machine stitch the piping to the fabric, using a zipper foot positioned right next to the stitching on the piping. Leave 3in (8cm) of piping unstitched at the end.

Cut notches into the seam allowance

3 Lay the cut ends of the piping on top of each other, then cut the piping casing to give a 1⅝in (4cm) overlap.

4 Open out each end of the piping casing, pull the piping cord out of the way, and hold the ends with the wrong side of each facing you. Leaving the left-hand end where it is, twist the right-hand end away from you so the right side of the casing is now facing you.

5 Holding the ends in this position, overlap them, left over right, so that the short end of the left-hand piece lines up with the long edge of the right-hand piece, and the corners match up. Pin from top to bottom, as shown.

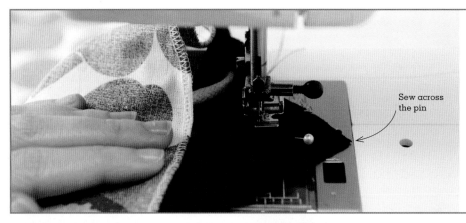

Sew across the pin

6 Machine stitch the two ends together horizontally across over the pin. Remove the pin and trim the raw edges of the seam to ⅜in (1cm).

7 With the casing opened out, overlap the ends of the piping cord and cut them level. Do not cut directly on top of the seam in the casing, since this leads to too much bulk. Tuck the ends of the cord inside the casing, then bring the raw edges of the casing together and machine stitch them closed.

Making the ties

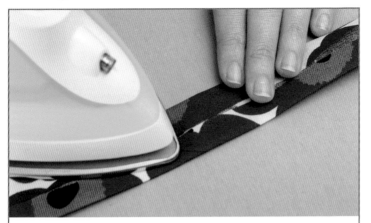

1 Cut a long strip the width of your fabric and 2⅜ in (6cm) wide. Fold in half lengthwise, wrong sides facing, then press. Open out, then fold the raw edges into the center fold. Press again. Cut into two equal lengths.

2 To neaten the ends, fold the ties right sides together in the opposite direction, with the raw edges pointing away from you. Pinch the ends together, matching the folded edges.

3 Machine stitch across each short end with a ⅜ in (1cm) seam allowance.

4 Turn the tie right side out and tuck in the ends.

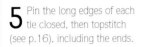

5 Pin the long edges of each tie closed, then topstitch (see p.16), including the ends.

6 Lay the top of the seat cushion right side up. Fold each tie in half and place the fold over the notches that mark the uprights, aligning the folded edge of the tie with the raw edges of the seat cushion and the piping. Lay the ends of the tie on top of the seat cushion, then slightly pull them apart, creating a "V." Machine stitch across the "V" within the seam allowance.

Inserting the zipper

1 With the zipper face down and open, center one of its sides between the ties. Position the teeth right on top of the piping. This will allow you to stitch close enough to cover the stitching in the casing. Fold back the loose end of the zipper tape and pin at 1¼in (3cm) intervals.

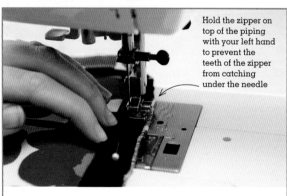

Hold the zipper on top of the piping with your left hand to prevent the teeth of the zipper from catching under the needle

2 Use a zipper foot and adjust the needle. Stitch the zipper in place, using your left hand to hold the teeth in position on top of the piping. Backstitch at the start and end of the seam to secure your stitching.

3 Fold the bottom of the seat cushion in half, then in half again and mark the halfway and quarter points with pins. Repeat for the top of the seat cushion.

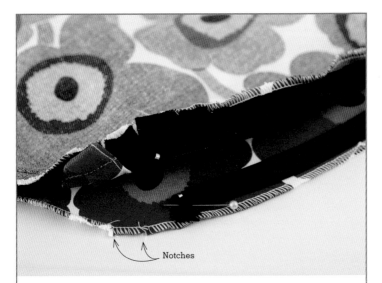

Notches

4 Lay the bottom of the seat cushion right side up and lay the top, with its zipper attached, right side down. Center the other side of the zipper between the notches on the bottom of the seat cushion. Ensure that the notches on the bottom of the seat cushion align with the ties on the top. Pin in place with the teeth of the zipper ⅝ in (1.5cm) from the edge and the excess tape folded back. Stitch as before.

5 Close the zipper, leaving a hand's width open. Working from the top of the seat cushion and with the ties tucked between the top and bottom, match the edges of both, first at the halfway points, then at the quarter-way points. Pin at these points, then pin the remainder of the edges together, easing in any excess fabric.

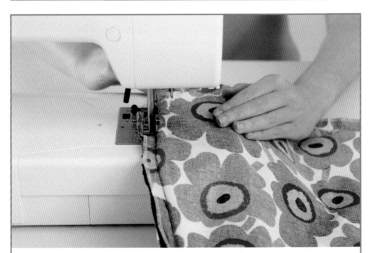

6 Using a zipper foot, having adjusted the needle and working from the top of the seat cushion so you can stitch closer to the piping, start machine stitching at one end of the zipper. Use the balance wheel to lower the needle and maneuver the fabric until the needle is as close to the end of the zipper as possible. Ensure that the zipper foot is close to the stitching line, then machine around the edges of the seat cushion, backstitching at the start to secure your stitching. Check regularly while you sew that the raw edges of the top and bottom of the seat cushion are aligned.

7 As you approach the end of the zipper, pull the end toward the seam allowance. Sew as close as possible to the end of the zipper, again using the balance wheel for accuracy. Backstitch several times to finish. Clip the curved seams, making sure you do not cut through your stitches. Turn the seat cushion to the right side and insert the foam.

Piped pouf

This pouf with attitude features a fabulous modern fabric and zingy contrasting piping. The zipper is hidden away underneath the pouf and is inserted in a similar way to the zipper in the Oxford pillow (see pp.32–35), but because sitting on the pouf puts strain on the zipper, some extra strengthening is required.

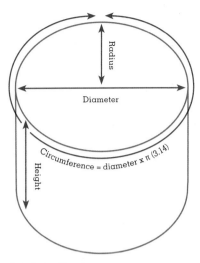

YOU WILL NEED

MATERIALS
- Muslin or cotton batiste for pattern, plus extra (optional) for lining
- Main fabric
- Matching thread
- Contrasting fabric for piping
- Contrasting thread
- Piping cord
- Filling (3–4 round pillow pads or feathers, polystyrene beads, or polyfill)

TOOLS
- Ruler
- Pencil
- Masking tape
- Compass or string
- Scissors
- Pins
- Sewing machine
- Iron
- Fabric pen
- Zipper foot
- Zipper, 2⅜in (6cm) shorter than the diameter of the pouf

Calculating the size
The diameter of your pouf should be the same as the diameter of your pillow pads. Figure out the circumference by multiplying the diameter by π (3.14). Decide the height according to the thickness of your filling.

Making a pattern and cutting out

Measure from the folded center point

1 Fold a square of muslin in half, then in half again. Calculate the radius of your pouf (half the diameter) and add a ⅝in (1.5cm) seam allowance. Measure and mark this distance on two adjacent sides of the muslin, starting at the folded center point.

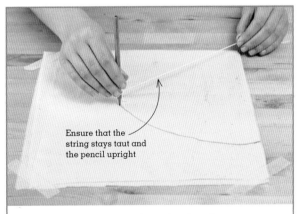

Ensure that the string stays taut and the pencil upright

2 Tape the folded muslin to the work surface. Use a compass to draw an arc from point to point or tie a pencil to a piece of string. Hold the pencil at one of the marks and, holding the string taut, pin the other end of the string to the folded center point. Hold the pencil upright at one mark and draw an arc to the second mark. Cut along the arc to cut out the pattern piece.

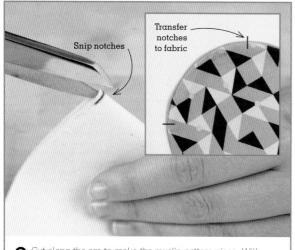

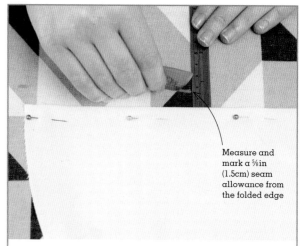

3 Cut along the arc to make the muslin pattern piece. With the muslin still folded, snip notches at the half and quarter points. Open the pattern piece and lay it on the main fabric. Pin and cut out, then transfer the notches to the fabric (inset). Neaten the edges of the fabric circle (see p.17). This is the top of your pouf.

4 For the base of the pouf, fold the pattern piece in half and place on the fabric. Measure and mark ⅝in (1.5cm) from the folded edge at several points. Join the marks. Cut the fabric out around the pattern piece, cutting the straight edge along the new line. Repeat to make a second base piece, but this time add 1in (2.5cm) along the folded edge. Mark and cut out as before.

5 You will now have two pieces for the base, one with an additional ⅝in (1.5cm) along its straight edge and the other with an additional 1in (2.5cm). Neaten the edges of the two pieces.

6 For the body of the pouf, cut a fabric rectangle with its long sides equal to the circumference of your pouf, plus two ⅝in (1.5cm) seam allowances, and with its short sides equal to the height of your pouf, plus two ⅝in (1.5cm) seam allowances. Neaten all the edges.

7 With right sides together, join the two short sides with a ⅝in (1.5cm) seam allowance to create a cylinder. Press the seam open. Fold the fabric cylinder in half and mark the half points with pins at the top and bottom edges. Fold in half again and mark the quarter points with pins (inset).

8 Stitch a line of ease stitching (see p.17) within the seam allowance and between the half and quarter markers on the body of the pouf, stopping and starting at each pin. This will help you to ease in any excess fabric when you come to assemble the pouf.

Inserting the zipper

Draw a 1¼in (3cm) line 1in (2.5cm) from the straight edge

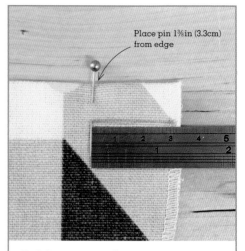

Place pin 1⅜in (3.3cm) from edge

1 With the smaller base piece face down, turn back then press the ⅝in (1.5cm) seam allowance. Turn the piece face up and unfold the seam allowance. Using a fabric pen, draw a 1¼in (3cm) line parallel to the fold line and 1in (2.5cm) from the straight edge. Repeat at the other end of the fold line. This is where the two base pieces will be stitched together.

2 Refold the 1.5cm (⅝in) seam allowance. Mark with a pin a second set of marks on both ends of the fold line at 1⅜in (3.3cm). This is where the zipper will go.

Draw a 1¼in (3cm) line along the fold line

3 With the larger base piece face down, turn back then press the 1in (2.5cm) seam allowance. Unfold the seam allowance and on the wrong side of the fabric, draw a 1¼in (3cm) line along the fold line from one end. Repeat at the other end of the fold line. Where the lines end, mark the right side of the fabric with dots.

Pin in place

1¼in (3cm) line

4 Place the smaller base piece face up. With the zipper face down and open, place one side of the zipper between the marks made in Step 2. Pin in place with the teeth just overhanging the fold line. Using a zipper foot and adjusting the needle so it is as close to the teeth of the zipper as possible, stitch the zipper in place.

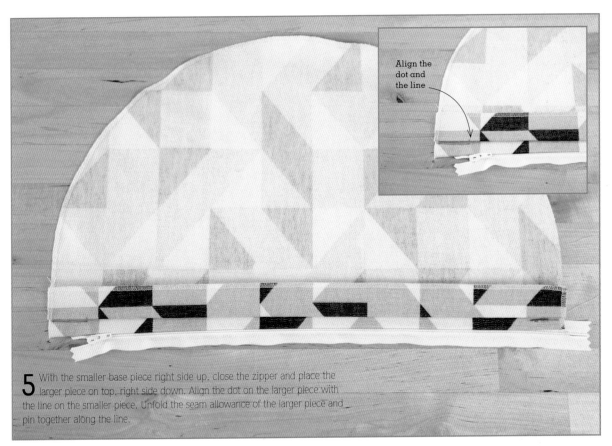

Align the dot and the line

5 With the smaller base piece right side up, close the zipper and place the larger piece on top, right side down. Align the dot on the larger piece with the line on the smaller piece. Unfold the seam allowance of the larger piece and pin together along the line.

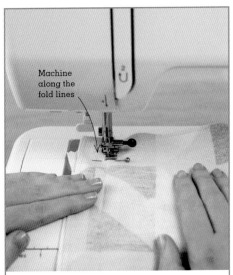

Machine along the fold lines

6 Machine stitch along the fold lines to join the two base pieces at either end of the zipper. Press the seam open.

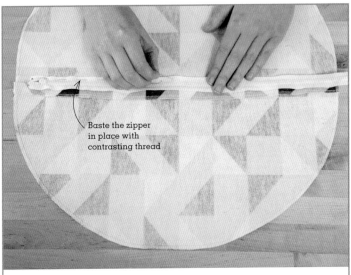

Baste the zipper in place with contrasting thread

7 Open the joined base piece flat and lay it wrong side up. Match the second side of the zipper to the neatened straight edge of the larger base piece. Baste the zipper in place through all the layers.

8 Working from the right side and using a medium-length stitch, stitch the zipper in place. Starting at the closed end of the zipper and backstitching to secure the thread, machine stitch across the short end of the zipper until the foot has cleared the teeth. Leave the needle down, lift the foot, and pivot to sew along the basted side of the zipper.

9 Sew along the length of the zipper, keeping the edge of the foot along the edge of the teeth. Stop at the end of the zipper, then pivot again and stitch along the other short end. Backstitch to secure.

Attaching the piping

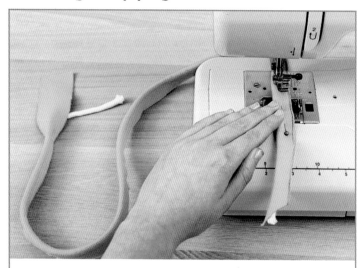

1 Make two lengths of piping (see pp.59–61) from the contrasting fabric, at least 1⅝in (4cm) longer than the circumference of the pouf. Leave 4in (10cm) of each end unstitched. Snip the seam allowance at ⅝in (1.5cm) intervals to ease the piping around the curves.

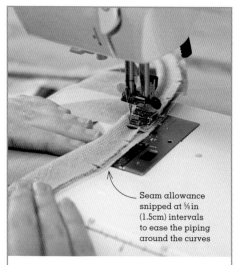

Seam allowance snipped at ⅝in (1.5cm) intervals to ease the piping around the curves

2 With right sides together, align the raw edge of the piping with the edge of the top of the pouf. Using a zipper foot, stitch as close to the piping cord as possible. Leave 4in (10cm) unstitched at the start and finish.

3 To join the ends of the piping, place the pouf top right side up, with the unstitched ends of the piping lying on top of each other. Measure and mark the casing to give an overlap of 1⅝in (4cm). Snip off the excess casing.

4 Open out each end of the piping casing and hold the ends with the wrong side of each facing you. Leaving the left-hand end where it is, twist the right-hand end away from you so the right side of the casing is now facing you.

5 Holding the ends in this position, overlap them, left over right, so that the short end of the left-hand piece lines up with the long edge of the right-hand piece, and the corners match up. Pin from top to bottom, as shown.

Stitch line

6 Machine stitch the two ends together across the pins. Remove the pins and trim the raw edges of the seam to ⅜ in (1cm).

7 With the casing opened out, overlap the ends of the piping cord and cut them level. Do not cut directly on top of the seam in the casing since it leads to too much bulk.

8 Tuck the ends of the cord inside the casing, then bring the raw edges of the casing together and machine stitch them closed. Repeat to attach piping to the bottom of the pouf.

Assembling the pouf

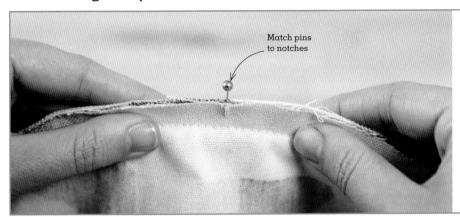

Match pins to notches

1 With right sides together, match the notches in the top of the pouf to the pins at the half and quarter points of the body. Pin at these four points first, then gently pull the ease stitches to ease the body to match the curve of the top of the pouf.

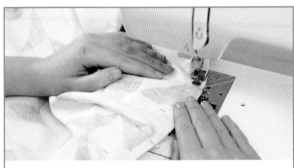

2 Pin in place then stitch along the seam allowance, as close to the piping cord as possible. Fold the bottom of the pouf in half, then in half again and mark the half and quarter points with pins. Open the zipper. Repeat Steps 1 and 2 to attach the bottom piece to the body.

3 Turn the pouf cover to the right side.

4 Either fill with a stack of round pillow pads or make a muslin lining consisting of two top pieces and one body piece. Fill the lining with feathers, polystyrene beads, or polyfill, and slip stitch closed.

Bench seat cushion

What could be more inviting to sit on than this deliciously plump cushion with its chic, contrasting piping? Make one and transform any bench or chest into a statement piece of furniture. The cushion gets its plump appearance from a layer of batting and stretch gauze fabric stitched around the foam pad.

YOU WILL NEED

MATERIALS
- Main fabric
- Contrasting fabric for piping
- Piping cord
- Upholstery zipper
- Foam
- Batting 1½ times the length of bench
- Stretch gauze fabric 2 times the length of bench
- Matching threads

TOOLS
- Scissors
- Ruler
- Tailor's chalk
- Sewing machine
- Pins
- Zipper foot
- Pencil

Side band

The side band wraps around the front and sides of the cushion. Depending on the width of your fabric you will almost certainly have to make it in three pieces—one long and two short. To calculate the length of the short pieces, add up one seat length and two seat widths to give the distance around the front and sides of the cushion (L + 2W). If the width of your fabric is less than this measurement you will need to add the difference as two pieces of equal length. Each piece will need its 2 x ⅝in (1.5cm) seam allowances all around.

CALCULATE THE CUTTING SIZES

Use the measurements of the foam pad to calculate the sizes of the fabric pieces you need to cut.

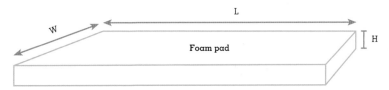

Foam

Choose the right thickness of foam for your project and have a piece cut to match the length (L) and width (W) of your bench. For a bench like this one, 4in (10cm) thick foam is a good choice. The height (thickness) of the foam is measurement H.

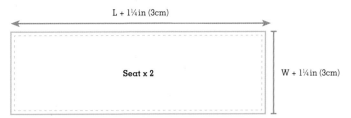

Top and bottom of seat

For these pieces, use the L and W measurements and add 1¼in (3cm) to each, giving you 2 x ⅝in (1.5cm) seam allowances along each side.

Zipper bands

The zipper bands sit on either side of the zipper along the back edge of the cushion. Their length is L + (2 x ⅝in/1.5cm) seam allowances and their width is ½H + (2 x ⅝in/1.5cm) seam allowances.

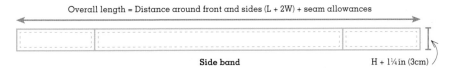

Cutting out

1 Lay out the fabric, wrong side up. Using your cutting sizes, measure and mark the length of the top of the seat along the width of the fabric, then mark the width. Repeat to mark the bottom of the seat, the side band pieces, and the zipper bands. Cut out all the pieces and neaten the edges (see p.17).

Sew as close to the cord as possible

2 Make the piping (see pp.59–61). You will need two continuous lengths of piping, each 2L + 2W + 1⅝in (4cm) long.

Attaching the piping

Leave the first 3⅛in (8cm) of piping unpinned

1 Lay the top of the seat on the work surface, right side up. Starting at a short edge, place the piping with its raw edge to the neatened edge of the top. Place the first pin 3⅛in (8cm) from the end of the piping.

Make a straight cut perpendicular to the piping

2 Continue pinning until ⅝in (1.5cm) before the corner. Snip a straight cut into the seam allowance of the piping at this point. Guide the piping around the corner. Continue pinning the piping around the rest of the seat top, snipping each corner in the same way.

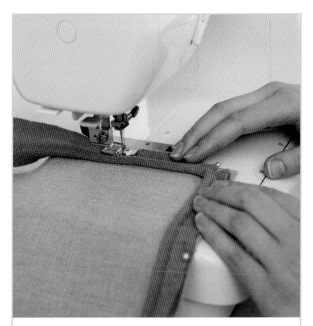

3 Leaving the first unpinned 3 ⅛ in (8cm) of piping free, machine stitch the piping to the seat top, using a zipper foot positioned right next to the stitching on the piping. Stitch up to the first corner.

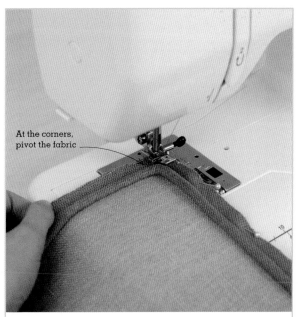

At the corners, pivot the fabric

4 Leaving the needle in the fabric, raise the presser foot and pivot the fabric, lower the foot, then continue stitching. Keep stitching around the seat top, and finish stitching 3 ⅛ in (8cm) before the end of the piping.

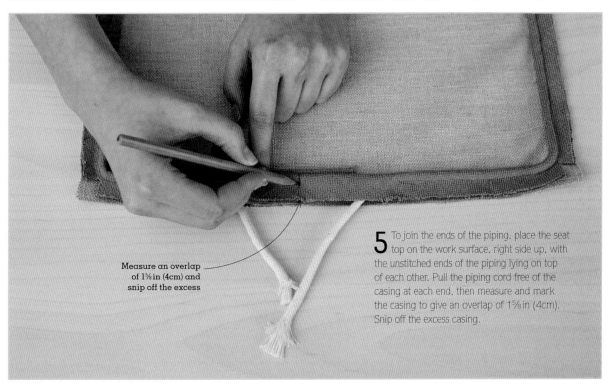

Measure an overlap of 1⅝ in (4cm) and snip off the excess

5 To join the ends of the piping, place the seat top on the work surface, right side up, with the unstitched ends of the piping lying on top of each other. Pull the piping cord free of the casing at each end, then measure and mark the casing to give an overlap of 1⅝ in (4cm). Snip off the excess casing.

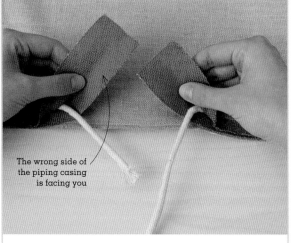

The wrong side of
the piping casing
is facing you

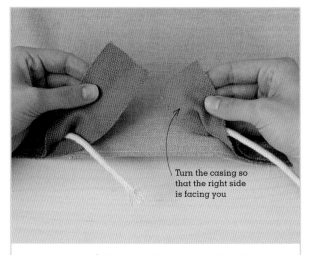

Turn the casing so
that the right side
is facing you

6 Still keeping the piping cord out of the way, open out each end of the piping casing and hold the ends with the wrong side of each facing you.

7 Leaving the left-hand end where it is, twist the right-hand end away from you so the right side of the casing is now facing you.

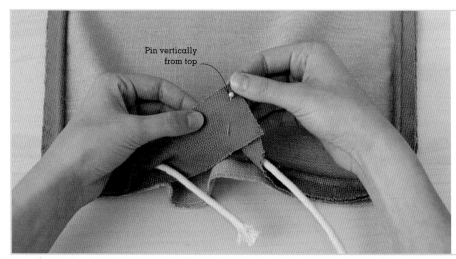

Pin vertically
from top

8 Holding the ends in this position, overlap them, left over right, so that the short end of the left-hand piece lines up with the long edge of the right-hand piece, and the corners match up. Pin from top to bottom, as shown.

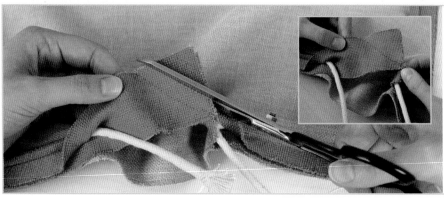

9 Machine stitch the two ends together, across the pin (inset). Remove the pin and trim the raw edges of the seam to ⅜ in (1cm).

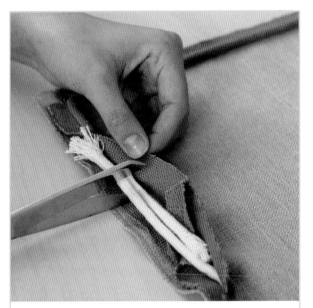

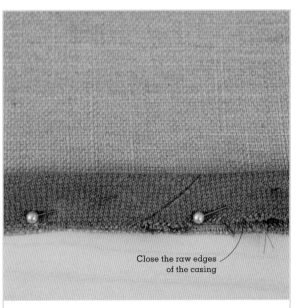

Close the raw edges
of the casing

10 With the casing opened out, overlap the ends of the piping cord and cut them level. Do not cut directly on top of the seam in the casing because this leads to too much bulk. Tuck the ends of the cord inside the casing.

11 Bring the raw edges of the casing together, pin, and stitch them closed. Check that the piping lies flat. Troubleshoot any wayward corners by making extra snips into the seam allowance of the piping until it lies flat. Repeat Steps 2–11 to add piping to the seat bottom.

Inserting the zipper

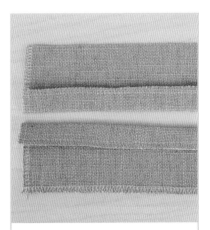

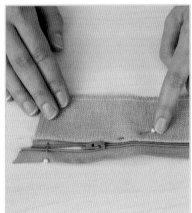

1 To assemble the side band, with wrong sides together and at a ⅝ in (1.5cm) seam allowance, join the short side of one small piece to one short side of the long piece. Next, join one short side of the other small piece to the other side of the long piece to make a continuous band.

2 Lay the zipper bands face down and press back a ⅝ in (1.5cm) seam allowance on each band. Cut a piece of zipper from the roll zipper so that it is slightly longer than the zipper bands.

3 Insert a zipper pull into the zipper (see p.22) and secure the ends of the zipper tape with a pin. Align the pressed edge of one of the zipper bands with the zipper teeth, as shown, and pin in place.

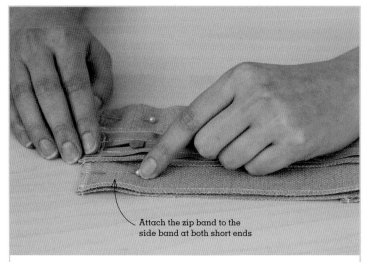

Attach the zip band to the
side band at both short ends

4 Using a zipper foot, stitch the zipper in place as close to the zipper as possible, while still leaving room for the zipper to open. Repeat to attach the other side of the zipper to the other zipper band.

5 Join the side band to the assembled zipper band. Place the pieces right sides together and pin one short end of the zipper band to one short end of the side band. Stitch together with a ⅝ in (1.5cm) seam allowance. Repeat at the other end to create a continuous side band. Press the seam allowances open.

Joining the pieces

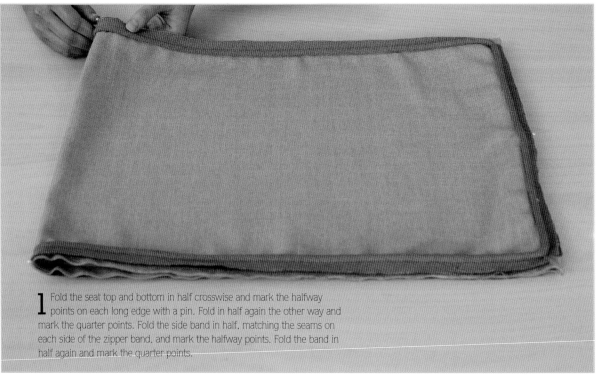

1 Fold the seat top and bottom in half crosswise and mark the halfway points on each long edge with a pin. Fold in half again the other way and mark the quarter points. Fold the side band in half, matching the seams on each side of the zipper band, and mark the halfway points. Fold the band in half again and mark the quarter points.

Match the center of the side band to the center of the seat top

2 With the pins as a guide, place the side band along the long side of the seat top, matching the half points. Repeat to match at the quarter points, then pin in place.

3 Using a zipper foot, stitch the band to the seat top. Sew with the piped side facing up to enable you to stitch close to the piping. When you reach a corner, snip the seam allowance of the band, leave the needle in the fabric, raise the presser foot, and pivot the fabric. Open the zipper, then repeat Steps 2–3 to attach the other edge of the side band to the seat bottom.

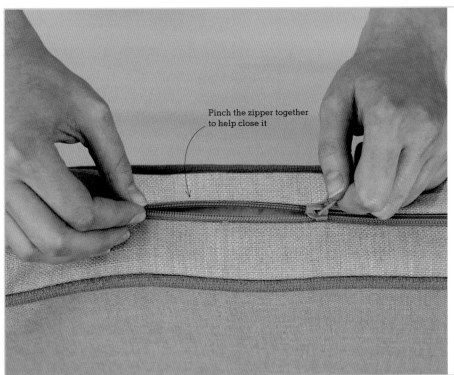

Pinch the zipper together to help close it

4 Turn the cover the right way out, pushing out the corners from the inside. Wrap the foam pad in a piece of batting, fold in the ends and secure with some loose basting stitches. To make it easier to insert it in the cover, wrap the batting-wrapped foam in stretch gauze fabric in the same way. Slip the foam into the cover and close the zipper to finish.

CURTAINS

Mix-and-match curtains

The place where you want to hang your curtains will dictate the qualities you want for them. By mixing and matching linings and heading styles, you can tailor your design to your room and your skill level.

Lining types

The lining you choose for a curtain will affect its weight, opacity, and insulating qualities, as well as how easy it is to make. Decide where your curtain will hang and what its primary use will be. For a bedroom you will probably want a lined curtain, to block light, but in a kitchen, an easy-to-wash, unlined curtain might be best.

UNLINED

Made from a single layer of fabric that is hemmed around the edges, unlined curtains are easy to make and will give a room an informal look. Although less lightproof, they are cheaper and easier to keep clean than lined curtains.

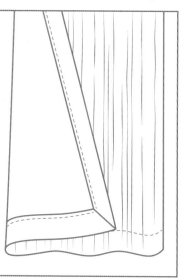

TUBE LINED

Making tube-lined curtains is simple and can easily be done on a sewing machine. The fabric and lining are joined together right side to right side along the long edges to form a tube. This technique is best used on smaller curtains.

INTERLINED

With an extra layer of material between the lining and the main fabric, interlined curtains are the thickest, heaviest option. This style involves hand sewing the lining to the main fabric along the long edges.

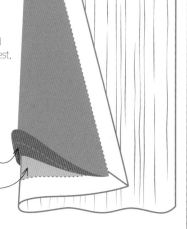

Lining

Interlining

SHEER

Sheer fabrics are normally extra-wide, often 3 ¼yd (3m), so they are ideal for making curtains to fit wide windows. You work with the selvages at the top and bottom, and cut the fabric to fit the width of the window, thus avoiding unsightly seams.

Curtain headings

Your choice of curtain heading not only affects the appearance of the top of the curtains, but also how they hang from their track or pole, and how easy they are to open and close. Some headings are more suitable for stationary curtains—those that are not opened and closed on a regular basis.

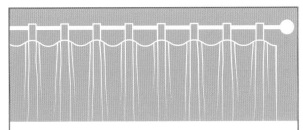

TAB TOP

Tab tops are a simple solution to hanging a curtain on a pole. They produce a modern look, though tab-top curtains can be more difficult than others to open and close. To measure the curtain length, measure from the very top of the pole.

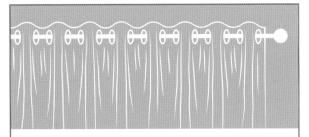

EYELET

Here the curtain pole is fed through reinforced eyelets to create a modern look. To measure the curtain length, measure from the very top of the pole and add ¾–1¼ in (2–3cm).

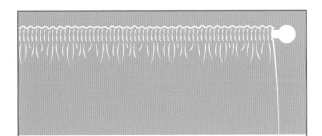

POCKET

In this style of heading, you sew a channel at the top of the curtain, into which you slide the curtain pole. The result is a gathered curtain. This heading is best for stationary curtains as the fabric can be difficult to move over the pole. To measure the curtain length, measure from the very top of the pole.

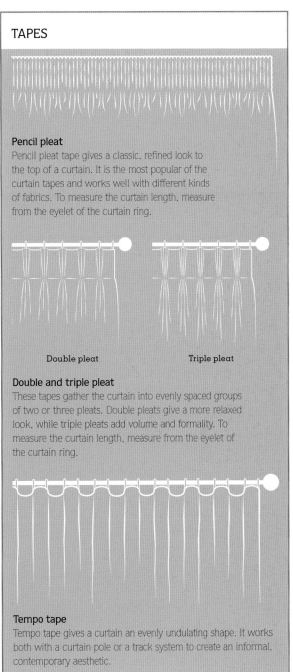

TAPES

Pencil pleat

Pencil pleat tape gives a classic, refined look to the top of a curtain. It is the most popular of the curtain tapes and works well with different kinds of fabrics. To measure the curtain length, measure from the eyelet of the curtain ring.

Double pleat   Triple pleat

Double and triple pleat

These tapes gather the curtain into evenly spaced groups of two or three pleats. Double pleats give a more relaxed look, while triple pleats add volume and formality. To measure the curtain length, measure from the eyelet of the curtain ring.

Tempo tape

Tempo tape gives a curtain an evenly undulating shape. It works both with a curtain pole or a track system to create an informal, contemporary aesthetic.

Making curtains

In addition to the heading style and lining, there are several things to consider when planning your curtains. The length of your curtains will influence everything from the overall appearance to the way the pattern is placed on the panels.

Curtain length

Curtain lengths can usually be classified into four types: sill-length, apron-length, floor-length, and pooling. Sill-length curtains sit ½in (1.2cm) above the windowsill. Apron-length curtains hit 2–4in (5–10cm) below the windowsill. Floor-length curtains just clear the floor by ½in (1.2cm). Finally, pooling curtains bunch on the floor with 2–8in (5–20cm) extra length, depending on your preference.

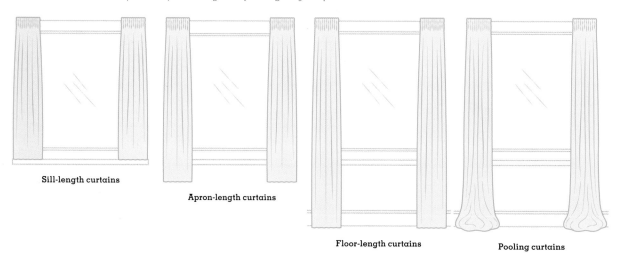

Sill-length curtains

Apron-length curtains

Floor-length curtains

Pooling curtains

Measuring for curtains

Always hang the pole or track before measuring to get an accurate measurement. The pole or track should be positioned about 6in (15cm) above the window and extend 6–8in (15–20cm) on either side of the window. Hanging an extra-wide curtain that extends more than 10in (25cm) on either side of the frame makes a smaller window look larger.

Use a metal tape measure for the most accurate measurements. Base your width measurements on the width of the pole or track, not of the window itself. Measure the total length of the track or pole, excluding finials, to get the curtain width. Then add an additional 1in (2.5cm) to this to allow for the curtains to overlap in the center when closed.

A curtain heading should sit slightly above a track so that the track is not visible. However, if using a curtain pole, the curtain should hang just below it so you see the pole.

For the length, decide which style you would prefer, as above. For sill- and apron-length curtains, measure from the pole or track to the windowsill, then add or subtract from this measurement depending on the style. For floor-length and pooling curtains, measure from the pole or track to the floor, then add or subtract from this measurement depending on the style. If in doubt, always overestimate, since you can always take up the length later.

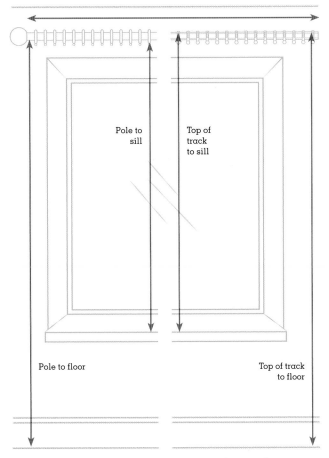

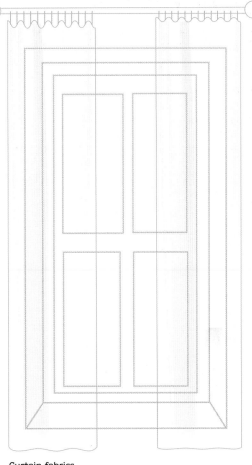

Hanging system length

Pole to sill

Top of track to sill

Pole to floor

Top of track to floor

Measuring for a pole
The spot you need to measure from will change depending on the type of curtain heading you've chosen (see p.107).

Measuring for a track
If using a track, measure from the top of the track so that the track will not be visible behind the hanging curtains.

Curtain fabrics
Sheers offer an attractive alternative to heavier curtains, especially during the summer months. They look particularly beautiful when they pool to the floor.

Curtain fullness and calculating fabric

Measure the track or pole and multiply by the fullness ratio, see right, which will vary depending on the type of heading. Divide this figure by the width of the fabric to be used and round up to the next whole number. This is the number of widths of fabric required for the pair of curtains. The number of widths of lining will be the same as the fabric.

Measure the finished length required. To calculate the cut length, add 8in (20cm) to the finished length for the hem allowances. If patterned fabric is used, extra will be needed for pattern matching. The length of the lining will be the same as the fabric, minus any extra for pattern matching.

To calculate the amount of fabric, lining, and interlining required for the curtains, multiply the number of widths by the cut length of the curtains.

Curtain style	Fullness ratio
Pencil pleat	2.00
Double pleat	2.30
Triple pleat	2.20
Gathered heading	1.80
Tab top	1.25
Tie top	1.25
Eyelet	1.50
Pocket top	1.00
Flat panel	1.00

Placing and matching a pattern

All patterned fabrics have a repeat down their lengths. This is called the pattern repeat and is measured from a point in one pattern to the same point in the next pattern. If using a patterned fabric you will need to match the pattern across the curtain panels and also across the seams if joining widths.

When joining widths, cut the first length of fabric to the required curtain length. Take note of the pattern at the top and locate this start point on the next uncut length of fabric. Place a pin at this point. Finger press back the selvage of the uncut length and maneuver the uncut piece until the pattern matches the first cut length at the selvage. Mark the top and bottom of the uncut length in line with the first cut length and cut across the fabric at the marks, at right angles to the selvage. Match the pattern across the two cut pieces along the selvage again. Secure with pins then slip stitch along the fold. Put right sides together, then machine stitch along the fold.

CALCULATING AMOUNTS OF FABRIC WITH PATTERN REPEATS

To calculate the amount of fabric you need, round the total cut length (see preceding page) to the nearest pattern repeat multiple, then multiply by the number of widths. For example, if the cut length is 52in (130cm) and the pattern repeat is 10in (25cm) you will need 60in (150cm), or six pattern repeats, per width of fabric. If you need four widths you will therefore need 240in (6m) of fabric in total.

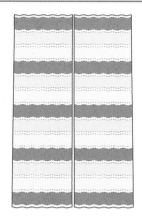

MATCHING ACROSS PANELS

Consider how the pattern will match across the curtain panels. Make sure the pattern will match edge-to-edge when the curtains are closed. Cut out the first curtain then match the second curtain to the first.

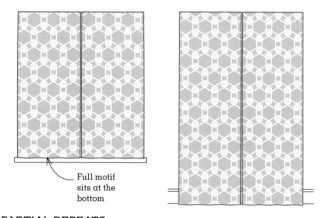

Full motif sits at the bottom

PARTIAL REPEATS

When placing a pattern it may be impossible to avoid a partial repeat at the top or the bottom. For sill- or apron-length curtains place the partial repeat at the heading. For floor-length or pooling curtains place the full pattern motif at the heading.

PLACING JOINS

When joining fabric width place narrower widths on the outer sides of the panels and the full width of the fabric in the center. Be sure to match the pattern across the seam.

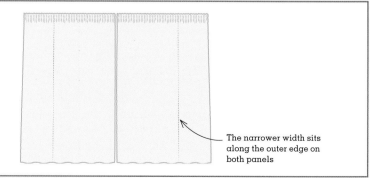

The narrower width sits along the outer edge on both panels

Header tapes

There are a number of different header tapes available for topping curtains, allowing you to create different looks, ranging from formal to modern. The pencil pleat photographed below, one of the most popular, is adaptable and suits many interior styles. Other tapes are attached in exactly the same way as the pencil pleat header tape.

Choosing your style

The curtains below are all made of the same fabric but look quite different because of their header tape. The tempo tape, soft and contemporary, is the most informal; the formal pinch pleat tape is suited to more traditional interiors.

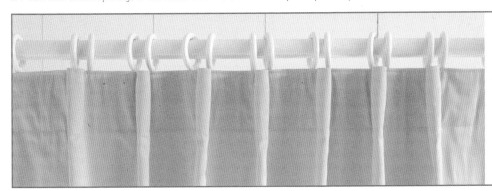

Cartridge tape
Cartridge tape forms small, rounded pleats separated by a flat panel. These can be pushed close together to give fullness to the curtain.

Tempo tape
Tempo tape is a relatively new header tape that guides the top of the curtain to form an S-shaped curve. It is best used on curtains that hang on a pole rather than a track to give the "S" plenty of space at the back.

Pinch pleat tape
Stylish and formal pinch pleats are made using a tape that creates groups of two or three pleats separated by a flat panel. Give the pleats additional structure by taking a few small stitches at the base of each group of pleats.

Cased-heading curtain

A sheer curtain panel with an ombré effect is a modern take on a traditional window treatment. Sheer fabrics are normally 118in (3m) wide, so here you have the selvages at the top and bottom of the curtain, while the sides start out as raw edges. Finish it off with a cased heading, one of the simplest ones to make.

YOU WILL NEED

MATERIALS

- Sheer or lightweight fabric
  (see p.109 for calculating amount)
- Matching thread
- ⅛in weighted drapery tape (length to match the width of your curtain)

TOOLS

- Pins
- Scissors
- Ruler
- Iron
- Serger (optional)
- Sewing machine
- Hand sewing needle
- Curtain rod

Squaring off the first side

1 Start by squaring off one long edge of the fabric. This will be one side of the finished curtain. With a sheer fabric or loose weave, as here, use a pin to pick out a single thread along the long edge.

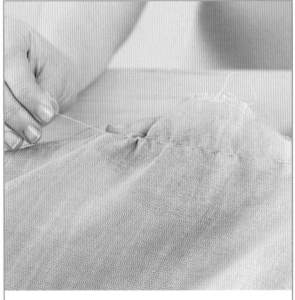

2 Gently pull the thread out completely, all the way along the long edge.

3 Cut along the line that is left where the thread was removed.

Neatening the sides

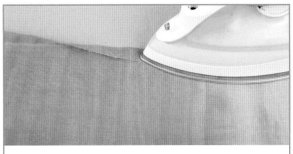

1 With the wrong side face up, fold over then press ⅝ in (1.5cm) along the long, straightened edge.

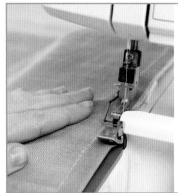

2 For a straight edge on a sheer fabric, use a serger. Turn off the knife and serge along the folded edge. If not using a serger, fold over and iron the edge a second time, then stitch close to the edge to create a double hem.

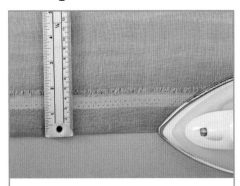

3 Trim the excess fabric from the edge. (Skip this if you have made a double hem.)

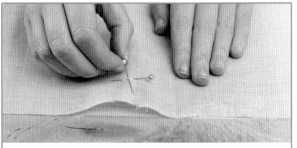

4 Measure across the fabric from the neatened edge to the width of your curtain (see p.108) and mark with a pin. Using a second pin, pull out a thread along the edge at this point. Cut along the line, then fold, press, and serge the edge, or create a double hem.

Making the hem

1 With the wrong side face up, fold over the selvage and press a 1⅝ in (4cm) hem along the bottom.

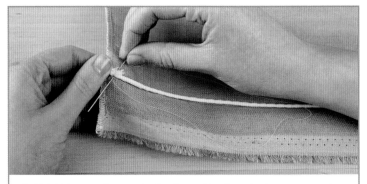

2 Unfold the hem. Remove the first few weights from the drapery tape and close the end of the tape with a few stitches. Stitch the end of the tape to one end of the fold line. Cut the tape to the width of the curtain and stitch the cut end to the other end of the fold line.

3 Fold the hem up so the selvage meets the drapery tape. Press the hem in place.

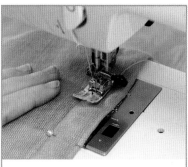

4 Turn the hem up again to make a double hem that encloses the drapery tape. Pin in place.

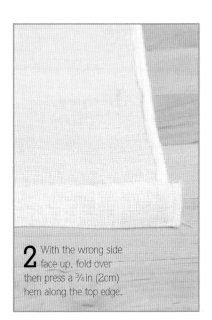

5 Stitch along the hem $^3/_{16}$ in (4mm) from the first folded edge. Press.

Making the cased heading

1 Lay the curtain flat. Measure the drop from top to bottom along the edges and the points across the width. Mark with pins. Fold over to the wrong side at the pinned line and press. Remove the pins. Mark a line $3^1/_4$ in (8cm) down from the fold across the width of the curtain. This makes a casing for a a rod up to $1^3/_8$ in (3.5 cm) in diameter. You may need to make it deeper for a thicker rod. Cut off the excess. Pin, iron, then cut along the fold.

2 With the wrong side face up, fold over then press a $^3/_4$ in (2cm) hem along the top edge.

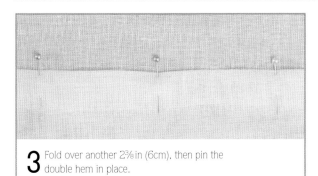

3 Fold over another $2^3/_8$ in (6cm), then pin the double hem in place.

4 Stitch along the hem close to the first folded edge to create the cased heading. Insert a curtain rod through the cased heading to hang your curtain.

Hanging play tent

A play tent suspended from the ceiling makes a comfortable den in a child's room where she can read undisturbed. It has its own curtain that can be closed or left open.

YOU WILL NEED

MATERIALS

- 10 yards (9m) lightweight cotton fabric for the tent
- Embroidery hoop or hula hoop (we used an embroidery hoop with an 18¾in (47cm) diameter)
- 60in (150cm) ribbon
- Matching thread
- White thread
- 40in (1m) fabric for the bunting
- 60in (1.5m) Velcro fastening tape

TOOLS

- Pencil
- Ruler
- String
- Masking tape (optional)
- Scissors
- Pins
- Sewing machine
- Iron
- Ceiling hook

Tent top

To calculate the size of the tent top, measure the diameter of the hoop and add a ⅝in (1.5cm) seam allowance.

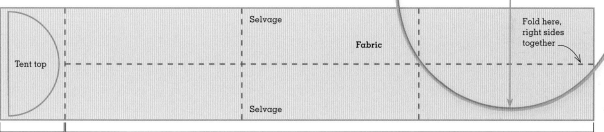

Making the tent top

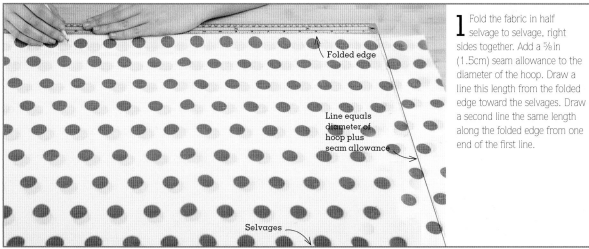

1 Fold the fabric in half selvage to selvage, right sides together. Add a ⅝in (1.5cm) seam allowance to the diameter of the hoop. Draw a line this length from the folded edge toward the selvages. Draw a second line the same length along the folded edge from one end of the first line.

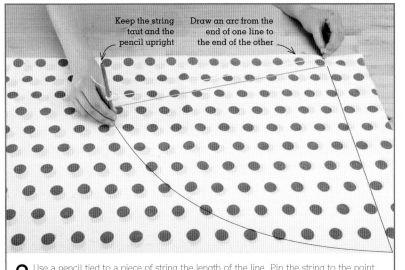

Keep the string taut and the pencil upright

Draw an arc from the end of one line to the end of the other

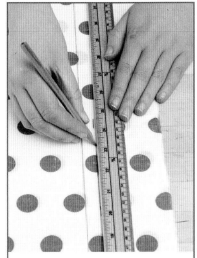

2 Use a pencil tied to a piece of string the length of the line. Pin the string to the point where the lines meet. Hold the pencil upright and draw an arc from the end of one line to the end of the other. Keep the string taut. It may help to tape the fabric to the work surface with masking tape to stop it from slipping.

3 Measure and mark a ⅝in (1.5cm) seam allowance along the first line. Cut through both layers of fabric to cut out the tent top.

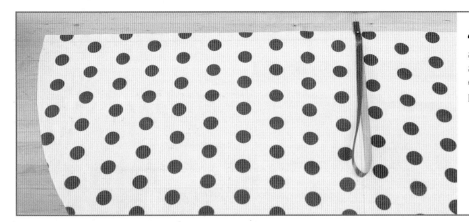

4 Open out the semicircular tent top, right side up. Cut a 20in (50cm) length of ribbon and fold it in half. Place the raw edges of the ribbon at the center point, as shown. Pin in place.

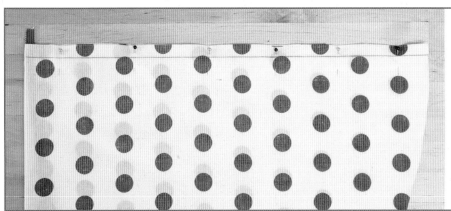

5 Fold the tent top right sides together with the ribbon tucked inside. Pin along the open, straight edge. Sew along the edge, starting at the ribbon, stitching over it, and backstitching a few times at the start to ensure the ribbon is stitched firmly in place. Press the seam open.

Making the tent body

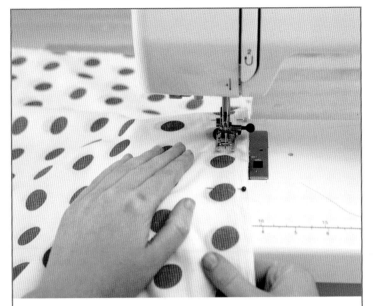

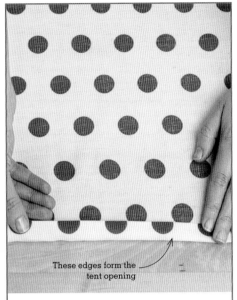

These edges form the tent opening

1 Cut the remaining fabric into three equal, full-width pieces for the tent body. Place two pieces selvage to selvage and right sides together. Pin and stitch with a ⅝in (1.5cm) seam allowance. Press the seam open. Attach the third piece to the other two in the same way. You now have three joined pieces with a selvage on both long edges.

2 With the fabric face down, turn over a ⅝in (1.5cm) double hem along the two selvages. Pin, then machine stitch in place as close to the edge as possible. Press to set the stitches. These edges form the opening.

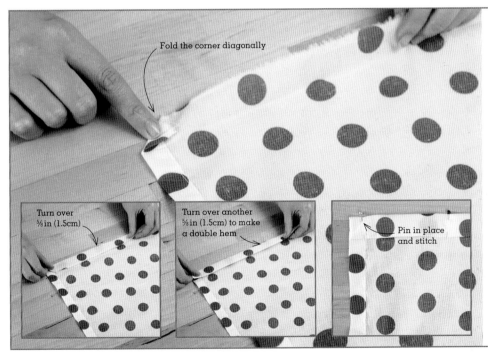

Fold the corner diagonally

Turn over ⅝in (1.5cm)

Turn over another ⅝in (1.5cm) to make a double hem

Pin in place and stitch

3 With the fabric face down, turn over a 1¼in (3cm) double hem all the way along the bottom of the three pieces (insets 1 and 2). At each end, miter the corner by folding it diagonally. Pin and stitch in place (inset 3). Press to set the stitches.

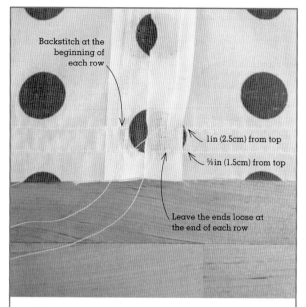

Backstitch at the beginning of each row

1in (2.5cm) from top

⅝in (1.5cm) from top

Leave the ends loose at the end of each row

4 Set the stitch length to its maximum length and machine stitch two rows of gather stitches along the top of each panel, stopping and starting at each seam. Stitch the first row ⅝in (1.5cm) from the top and the second 1in (2.5cm) from the top. Backstitch at the beginning of each row but not at the end.

5 Now you will need to gather the fabric. To do this, hold the pair of loose threads at the end of the row in one hand. With the other hand, push the fabric away from you.

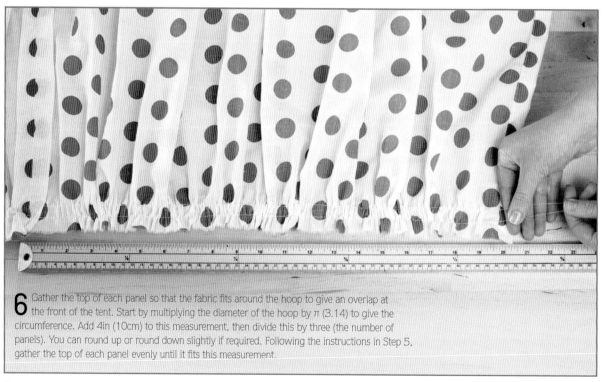

6 Gather the top of each panel so that the fabric fits around the hoop to give an overlap at the front of the tent. Start by multiplying the diameter of the hoop by π (3.14) to give the circumference. Add 4in (10cm) to this measurement, then divide this by three (the number of panels). You can round up or round down slightly if required. Following the instructions in Step 5, gather the top of each panel evenly until it fits this measurement.

7 Secure the ends of the gather stitches on each panel by wrapping them around a pin in a figure eight.

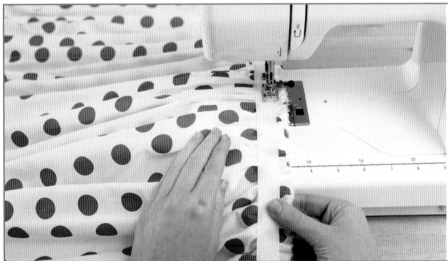

8 Cut a length of looped Velcro tape to match the hoop's circumference. Place the gathered fabric under the machine foot, right side up. Lay the Velcro tape on top, aligning its top edge with the upper row of gather stitches, as shown here. Stitch the Velcro in place along its top edge, ensuring that the gathers remain even and keeping them at a right angle to your stitches. Stitch along the bottom edge of the Velcro tape, starting from the same end as before.

9 Cut five lengths of ribbon 12in (30cm) long and mark the middle of each. Lay the gathered tent body face down. Space the ribbons out evenly along the gathered edge and pin in place through the middle of each ribbon. Hand or machine stitch in place.

Joining top and bottom

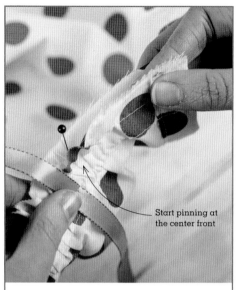

1 Stay stitch (see p.17) around the bottom edge of the tent top. With wrong sides together, lay the tent top flat with the seam to one side. Mark the side opposite the seam with a pin. This is the center front of the tent.

2 With right sides together, pin the body of the tent to the top. Starting at the center front of the top, pin in the body so it overlaps the center front of the top by 2in (5cm).

Start pinning at the center front

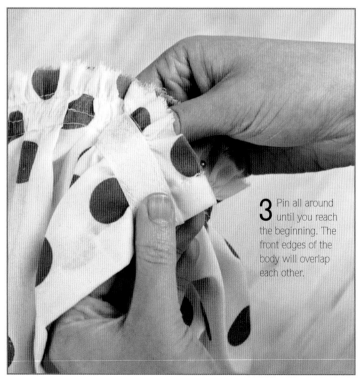

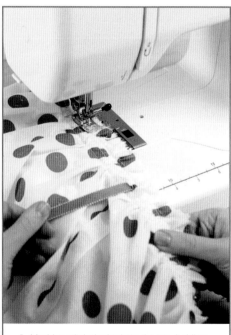

3 Pin all around until you reach the beginning. The front edges of the body will overlap each other.

4 Machine stitch the body to the top, holding the ribbons out of the way of the needle.

Making the bunting

Mark lines at top and bottom

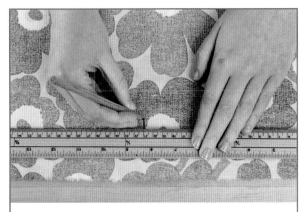

1 Cut two strips of bunting fabric, each 12in (30cm) deep and long enough to fit the circumference of the hoop. If necessary, make each strip from two pieces joined right side to right side along the short edge. Place the two long strips right sides together. Draw a line ⅜in (1cm) from the bottom edge and a second line 2in (5cm) from the top.

2 An ideal width for what will be the top of a flag is 8in (20cm). Calculate how many times this will fit around your hoop. Adjust the width until it divides into the circumference of the hoop evenly. Mark the width of the first flag along the line. Mark the same amount for the next flag and so on until you reach the end.

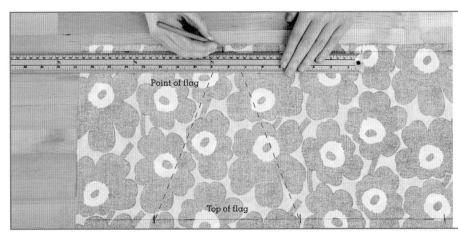

Point of flag

Top of flag

3 Mark the points of the flags on the bottom line. Starting at the bottom left-hand edge, mark 4in (10cm) along the line, then a further 8in (20cm), followed by 8in (20cm) each time until you reach the end.

4 To mark the outlines of the flags, start at the left-hand edge and join the end of the top line with the first mark on the bottom line. Continue joining marks diagonally. Then join them in the other direction.

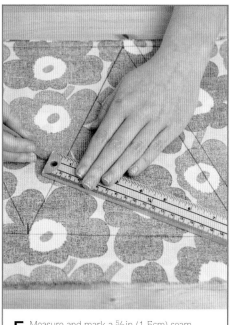

5 Measure and mark a ⅝in (1.5cm) seam allowance along the outer edges of each flag, as shown.

6 Pin or baste both layers together. Cut out through both layers around the seam allowances, removing the excess fabric as you go.

7 Sew along the seam allowance lines in one continuous seam, pivoting at the corners.

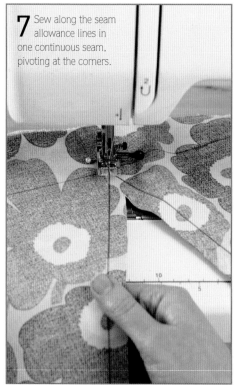

8 Snip between the flags close to the seam allowance but make sure you do not cut through your stitches.

9 Trim off the seam allowance around the points of the flags as close as possible to the stitching.

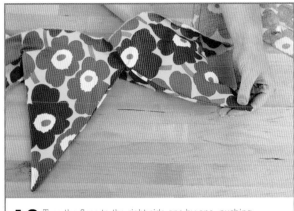

10 Turn the flags to the right side one by one, pushing the points of the flags out using a pointed but blunt tool such as a pencil.

11 Lay the bunting flat on the table, finger-pressing the seams to the sides. Check that the joins between the flags lie flat, clipping into the seam allowances a little more if necessary. Press the bunting.

12 Fold over ⅜in (1cm) at the top of the band.

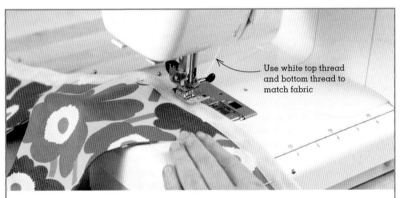

Use white top thread and bottom thread to match fabric

13 Lay a length of hooked Velcro, right side up, on the folded band. Pin then stitch the Velcro tape along its top edge, then along the bottom edge, starting from the same end as before.

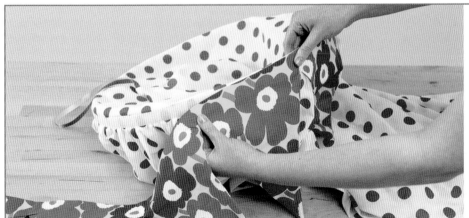

14 Tie the hoop inside the tent using the ribbons around the body. Attach the bunting to the outside using the Velcro tape. Hang the tent up from a ceiling hook.

Tab-top curtain

Unlined and informal, a tab-top curtain is simplicity itself to make. As with all sewing projects, the key is to measure, then measure again to double-check. Before you start to cut your fabric, decide on the position of your pole. Placing it well above the window or door frame, as here, will make your room look bigger.

YOU WILL NEED

MATERIALS
- Fabric
- Matching thread
- Drapery weights
- Small piece of muslin

TOOLS
- Triangle
- Tape measure
- Tailor's chalk
- Scissors
- Iron
- Pins
- Sewing machine
- Hand sewing needle

CUTTING LENGTH

The finished tab, from the top of the pole to the top of the curtain, is 2⅜in (6cm). To calculate the cutting length of the curtain fabric, measure from the top of the pole to the required drop. Deduct the length of the tab from this measurement, then add 4in (10cm) for the hem and 2¾in (7cm) for the header.

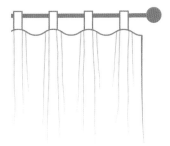

Pin double hem before stitching

Tab-top curtain
One of the easiest curtain headers to make, the tabs of a tab-top header are made in either matching or contrasting fabric and sewn to the top edge of the curtain.

Unlined curtain
Made from a single layer of fabric that is hemmed all around, an unlined curtain is quick and easy to make. We add drapery weights to ensure that the curtain hangs smoothly and looks sharp.

Measuring and cutting

1 Lay the fabric on the work surface right side up. Square off the bottom (see p.15) and cut off the excess.

2 Figure out the cutting length, as outlined above. Measure from the bottom edge to this length and cut out.

Making the tabs

1 You will need eight tabs per standard width of fabric. Cut each one 10 x 2¾in (25 x 7cm) wide. Fold each tab in half lengthwise, wrong sides facing, then press. Open out.

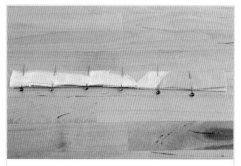

2 Press a ⅜in (1cm) seam allowance toward the fold along each long edge. Refold along the center, matching the folded edges. Pin.

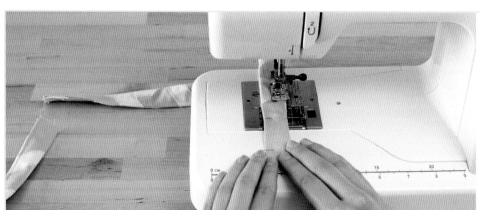

3 Topstitch (see p.16) along each long side of the tab, as close to the edge as possible. To save time, you can stitch all the tabs in one continuous chain, then cut through the stitches holding them together.

Hemming the sides and bottom

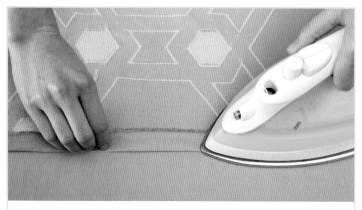

1 With the wrong side of the curtain face up, fold over then press 1in (2.5cm) along the sides of the curtain. Repeat to make a double hem.

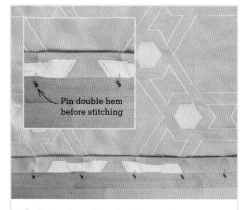

Pin double hem before stitching

2 Pin in place, then stitch close to the folded edge.

3 With the wrong side face up, fold over 2in (5cm) along the bottom.

4 Fold over another 2in (5cm) to make a double hem. Pin in place.

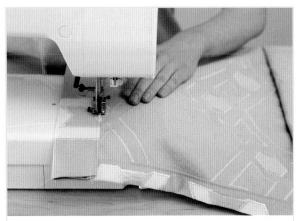

5 Stitch close to the folded edge, leaving the final 1in (2.5cm) unstitched at either end. Press the side and bottom hems.

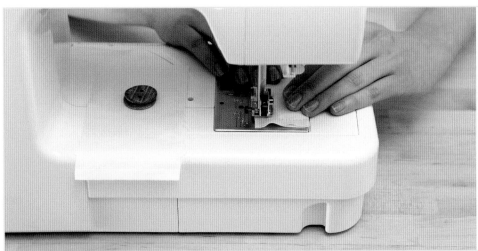

6 Machine-made curtains sometimes pull at the corners. Compensate for this by placing one or two drapery weights at each end of the bottom hem. Cut a muslin rectangle to fit around each pair of weights. Fold and stitch around three sides to form a small pouch.

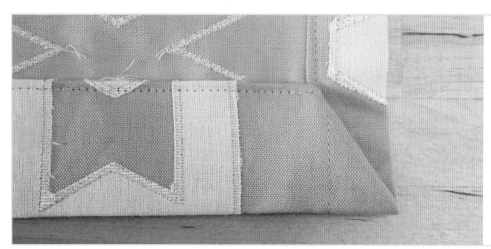

7 At each end of the bottom hem, fold in the unstitched fabric at an angle, as shown.

8 Tuck the covered weights into the hem, just behind the fold.

9 Slip stitch (see p.18) the fold closed, catching the muslin pouch in your stitching. Take care not to stitch through to the front.

Attaching the tabs

1 Fold a tab in half crosswise. With the right side of the curtain face up, pin the raw edges of the tab at one end of the curtain's top edge. Repeat to pin a second tab at the other end. Measure the distance between the tabs and divide by seven. Measure this amount from the first tab, then from the next, and so on. Place a pin at each of these points.

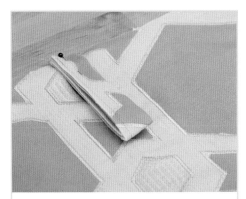

2 Pin a folded tab at each of the marked points. The tabs should be equally spaced.

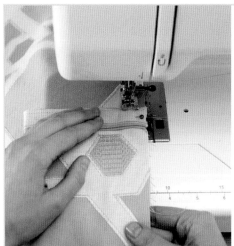

3 Machine stitch along the top edge of the curtain with a ⅝in (1.5cm) seam allowance, through all the pinned tabs. As you stitch, make sure the tabs remain perpendicular to the top edge. When you come to each tab, you may need to lift the presser foot and lower it again to stop the tabs from being pushed out of alignment by the foot.

4 With the wrong side of the curtain face up, turn the top edge over with the tabs attached along the stitching line. Press.

5 Turn the top of the curtain over by 2in (5cm). Pin in place.

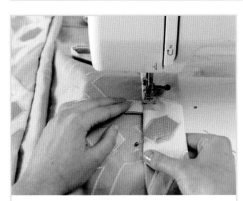

6 Stitch ⅜in (1cm) from the folded edge, removing the pins as you go.

7 Flip the tabs over the hem as shown and secure with a pin, then stitch ⅜in (1cm) from the top edge of the curtain, securing the tabs in your line of stitches. You may need to raise the foot as before. Insert a pole through the tabs to hang your curtain.

Curtain tiebacks

Complete any curtain with a tieback to hold it away from the window and allow maximum light to flood in to a room. A traditional, buckram-lined tieback like ours looks professional and tailored. You should be able to make a pair in just a few hours.

YOU WILL NEED

MATERIALS
- Tieback buckram (2 x ready-made or two pieces cut from buckram using the template on pp.208–209)
- Main fabric (large enough for two tiebacks plus 1in (2.5cm) seam allowance all around)
- Backing fabric (either matching fabric or lining fabric) the same size as the buckram
- 4 x D-rings or curtain rings, about 1in (2.5cm) diameter
- 2 x tieback hooks

TOOLS
- Scissors
- Pencil
- Pins
- Ruler
- Sewing machine
- Hand sewing needle

Tieback template
Use the template on pp.208–209 to create a tieback template the right size for your curtains

DECIDING THE SIZE OF A TIEBACK
A tieback must be long enough to hold the curtain back without bunching it up too much, so its length is determined by the number of fabric widths in the curtain and how bulky the material is. Measure around the gathered curtain to find the ideal length. The width of the tieback is also important: very short curtains look wrong with very wide tiebacks and, conversely, very long curtains don't fit well with narrow tiebacks. Usually the width varies between 4in (10cm) and 6in (15cm).

Measuring and cutting out

1 Lay two pieces of the main fabric face down on top of each other. If the fabric has a pattern, make sure that the pattern matches on both pieces. Place the tieback buckram on top, ensuring that it is symmetrical with any pattern.

2 Using a ruler and pencil, measure and mark a 1in (2.5cm) seam allowance all around the buckram. This wide seam allowance helps to support the curved edge and makes it easier when turning the tieback to the right side.

3 Remove the buckram and cut through both layers of fabric to cut out the two pieces. Cut two matching pieces from the backing fabric.

Assembling the tieback

1 Place one piece of backing fabric and one piece of main fabric right sides together.

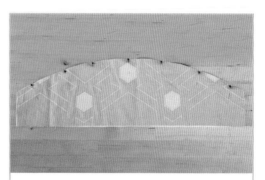

2 Pin along the curve.

3 Mark a dot 1in (2.5cm) from the long straight edge and 1in (2.5cm) from the short straight edge at each end.

4 Machine stitch from dot to dot along the curve with a 1in (2.5cm) seam allowance.

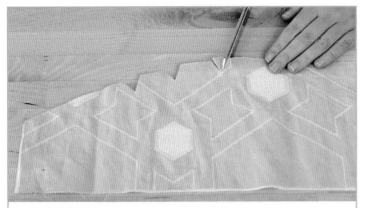

5 Cut notches into the seam allowance all the way around the curve, but make sure you do not cut through your stitches. Snip off the corners to reduce the bulk.

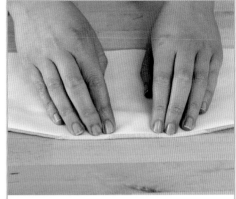

6 Turn the tieback to the right side. Roll the seam with your fingers to ease it to the edge and press.

7 Insert the buckram between the fabric and the backing.

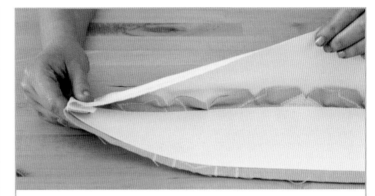

8 For a smooth finish, make sure that all the seam allowance fabric is facing the tieback backing.

9 Turn the edge of the main fabric under, then fold the edge of the backing fabric under until the two edges are aligned.

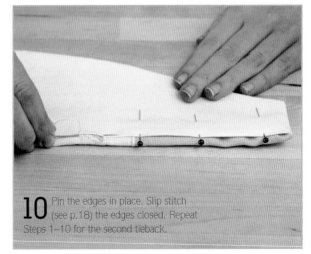

10 Pin the edges in place. Slip stitch (see p.18) the edges closed. Repeat Steps 1–10 for the second tieback.

Attaching the rings

1 One short edge of the tieback will be at the front and the other at the back. For the back, position the straight edge of a D-ring ⅜in (1cm) from the edge so the curved edge overhangs.

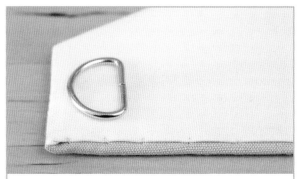

2 For the front, position the straight edge of a D-ring 1in (2.5cm) from the edge so the curved edge is on the tieback.

3 Oversew the rings in place at two points on their straight edge.

4 Make the second tieback in the same way. Switch the positions of the rings to make the tieback a mirror image of the first.

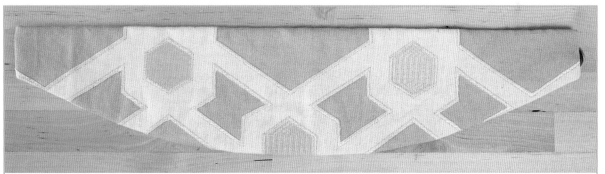

5 Position the tieback hooks at the required height on either side of the window. Loop the back end of the tieback on the hook, gather up the curtain, then loop the front end on the hook.

Lined eyelet curtain

With their contemporary, somewhat masculine look, eyelet curtains are a great choice for a room where you don't want a fussy window treatment. An added bonus is that their tubelike folds do not require a lot of fabric. If using a metal curtain pole, be sure to match its finish to the eyelet rings.

YOU WILL NEED

MATERIALS
- Main fabric (see pp.108–10 for quantity)
- Lining fabric (see pp.108–10 for quantity)
- Matching thread
- Eyelet tape and rings the width of the finished curtain, plus at least 8in (20cm)

TOOLS
- Triangle (optional)
- Tailor's chalk
- Scissors
- Pins
- Ruler
- Sewing machine
- Iron
- Tape measure
- Pencil

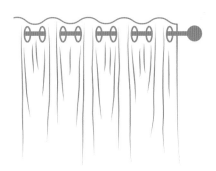

Eyelet heading
The eyelet heading tape is stitched across the top of the curtain. The eyelets are cut out and the backs of the rings are attached.

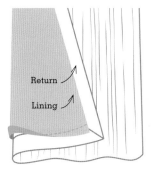

Lined curtain
These curtains are "tube lined"—a technique for making lined curtains using a sewing machine in which the main fabric and lining are stitched together right side to right side to form a tube.

Cutting the main fabric and making the hem

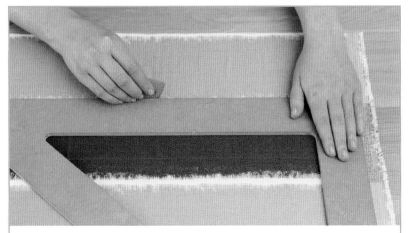

1 Lay the main fabric on the work surface right side up. Square off the bottom (see p.15) and cut off the excess. Starting from the bottom edge, use tailor's chalk and a tape measure to measure and mark the finished drop (see p.108 for measuring the drop) plus 6¾in (17cm) at several points across the width. Join the marks and cut along the line.

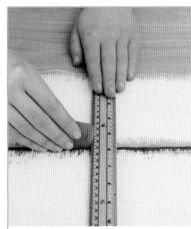

2 With the fabric face down, measure and mark 5⅝in (14cm) from the bottom edge at several points across the width, as before.

3 Join the chalk marks with a line. Fold the fabric to meet the line and press the fold.

4 Fold the edge of the fabric under by 2¾in (7cm) to create a double hem and press.

5 Secure the double hem with pins.

6 With the fabric face down, align the folded edge of the hem with the edge of the presser foot. Move the needle to the left. Using a medium-length stitch and the foot as a guide, stitch along the hem. Backstitch at the beginning and end of the seam to secure the stitches.

7 Fold the fabric in half lengthwise, right sides together, and mark the center points top and bottom with pins.

8 If the selvages are very wide, trim them off. Measure the new width of the fabric.

Hemming and attaching the lining

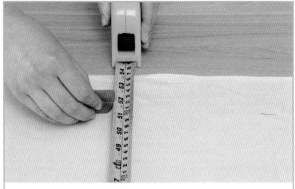

1 Subtract 3⅝in (9cm) from the new width of the main fabric. Starting from one long edge, measure and mark this amount at several points along the length of the lining.

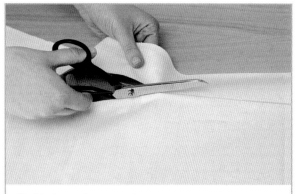

2 Join the marks and cut along the line. The lining is now 3⅝in (9cm) narrower than the curtain, which will create the returns (see p.137).

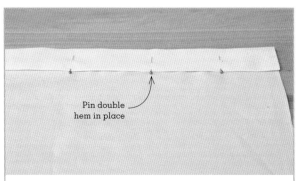

Pin double hem in place

3 With the lining face down, start from the bottom and measure 4in (10cm) at several points across the width. Join the marks with a line. Fold the fabric to the line and press. Fold under 2in (5cm) to make a double hem and press. Secure with pins, machine stitch, then press.

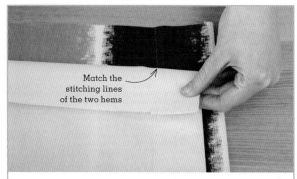

Match the stitching lines of the two hems

4 Fold the lining lengthwise and mark the center points top and bottom with pins. Place the main fabric and the lining right sides together, aligning the hem stitching lines of both pieces. The bottom of the lining should lie ¾in (2cm) above the bottom of the main fabric.

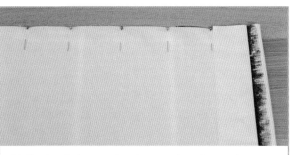

5 Keeping the hem stitching lines together, align one long edge of the lining with one long edge of the main fabric. Pin along the edge.

6 The main fabric will now extend beyond the other long edge of the lining because the lining is narrower.

7 Fold the long edge of the lining back, then make a fold in the main fabric from top to bottom, as shown.

8 Unfold the long edge of the lining and align it with the long edge of the main fabric. The fold in the main fabric will be tucked under the lining. Smooth out the lining, check the hem stitching lines are still aligned, and secure with pins along the long edge.

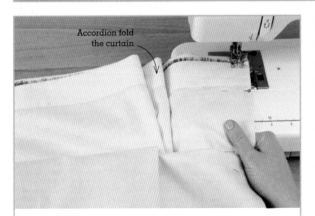

Accordion fold the curtain

9 Accordion fold the curtain to make it easier to manage. With the curtain face down, align one long edge with the ⅝ in (1.5cm) marker on the needle plate (see p.16). Using a smaller length stitch and starting from the hemmed edges, stitch the long edges together, following the marker and backstitching at the beginning and end of the seam.

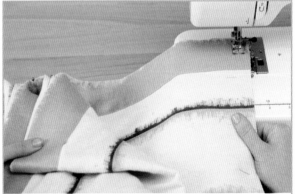

10 Turn the curtain over so it is face up and accordion fold it again. Stitch the other long edges together, again starting at the hemmed edges. The curtain and lining now form a tube.

11 Lay the curtain tube on the ironing board. Maneuver the seams so that they are not at the edges of the tube, then press both seam allowances toward the main fabric along both seams. This will encourage the seam allowances to lie flat when the curtain is turned to the right side.

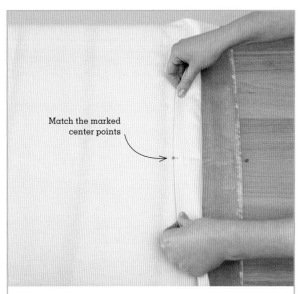

Match the marked center points

12 Turn the curtain to the right side and place on the work surface with the main fabric face down. Match the center points of the main fabric and the lining, top and bottom, keeping the hem stitching lines aligned. Pin together at the center points.

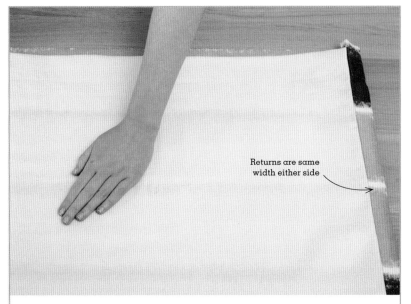

Returns are same width either side

13 Smooth out the curtain from the center to the edges. The same width of main fabric—the returns—should now be visible along either edge and the seam allowances should lie flat under the returns. Iron the edges of the returns into sharp folds.

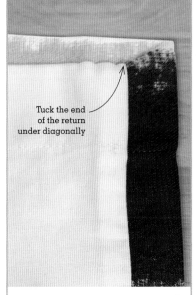

Tuck the end of the return under diagonally

14 At the bottom edge of the curtain, fold the hem of each return diagonally, tucking it under the return. This creates a half miter. Slip stitch (see p.18) into place.

Attaching the eyelet tape

1 Starting from the hem of the main fabric, measure and mark the finished drop at several points across the width. Turn the main fabric over the lining along the marks and press. Baste (see p.18) in place.

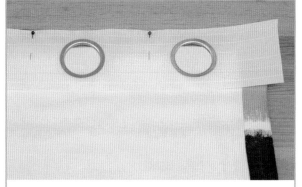

2 Place the eyelet tape so its top edge is a little way beneath the top edge of the curtain and the first and last eyelets are equidistant from each long edge. Pin in place. Trim off the excess tape, leaving a ¾in (2cm) overhang at each long edge.

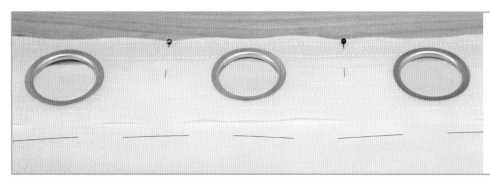

3 To hold the layers together, sew a line of basting stitches through all the layers of fabric just below the eyelet tape.

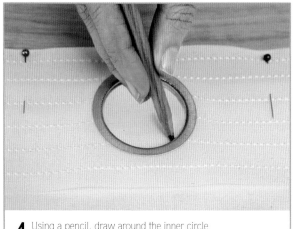

4 Using a pencil, draw around the inner circle of each eyelet.

5 Remove the eyelet tape. Using the tip of the scissors, snip into each circle and cut to the edge in both directions. Snip across at right angles to the first cut.

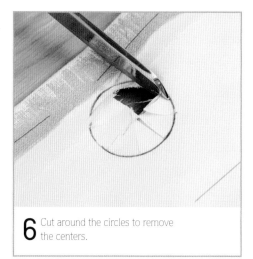

6 Cut around the circles to remove the centers.

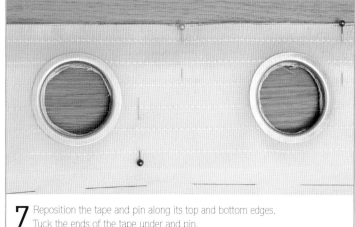

7 Reposition the tape and pin along its top and bottom edges. Tuck the ends of the tape under and pin.

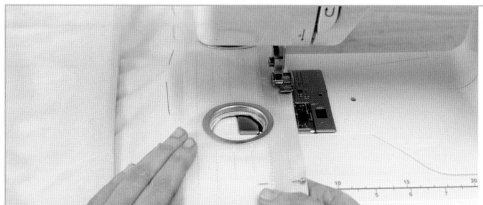

8 Stitch the tape in place through all the layers along a short edge, then pivot and stitch along a long edge. Stitch along the other long edge, then pivot to stitch the other short edge. Stitch both long edges in the same direction to prevent puckering.

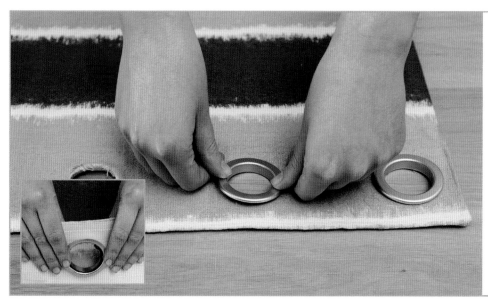

9 Insert the front of each ring through the front of the curtain and snap the front and back together (inset). Insert your curtain pole through the rings to hang the curtain.

Pencil pleat curtain

Crisp without being formal, pencil pleats are easily formed at the top of a curtain using the appropriate header tape. Other header tapes are attached in exactly the same way—see p.111 for more options. This pair of curtains is interlined as well as lined, which gives a beautiful, professional finish.

YOU WILL NEED

MATERIALS
- Main fabric (see pp.108–10 for quantity)
- Lining fabric (see pp.108–10 for quantity)
- Interlining fabric (see pp.108–10 for quantity)
- Pencil pleat header tape, to fit the width of the ungathered curtains
- Matching thread

TOOLS
- Ruler/yardstick
- Triangle
- Scissors
- Hand sewing needle
- Sewing machine
- Iron
- Pins
- Tailor's chalk
- Tape measure
- Curtain hooks
- Drapery weights

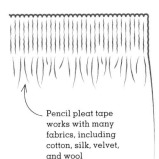

Pencil pleat tape works with many fabrics, including cotton, silk, velvet, and wool

Pencil pleat heading
A pencil pleat header tape is stitched across the top of the curtain to create narrow pleats.

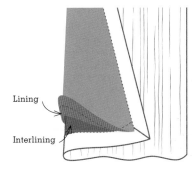

Lining

Interlining

Interlined curtain
The curtains are draft-proof and lusciously thick thanks to the interlining that is stitched to the main fabric. The lining fabric is hand-stitched in place along the edges of the returns.

Cutting the fabric and preparing the hem

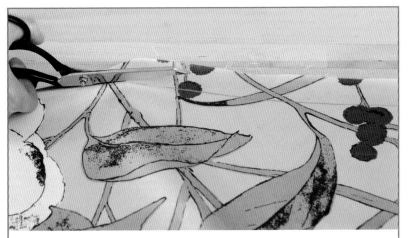

1 Measure the cutting size for your curtains (see pp.108–110). Square off the fabric along the bottom edge (see p.15). Cut the fabrics and interlining to the required size for each curtain. If more than one width is required, join the widths together with a flat seam. Make sure to add any half-widths at the outside edges (see p.110 for joining panels).

Selvage of main fabric

2 Place the main fabric on the work surface face down and lay the interlining on top. Match the raw edges along the sides and the bottom.

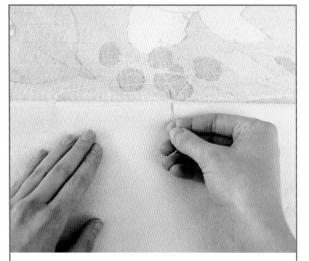

3 To hold the interlining in place, fold back its long edge by 8in (20cm). Using matching thread, use locked whipstitch (see p.19) to join the interlining to the main fabric from top to bottom along the folded edge, spacing the stitches approx 4in (10cm) apart and stopping them about 4in (10cm) short of the bottom edge. Repeat along the other long edge. (If your curtain is more than one width wide, also whipstitch the interlining to the main fabric along each seam.)

4 Unfold the whipstitched edge, then, with the main fabric still face down, fold the two fabrics over together by 2in (5cm). This is called a return. Starting 14in (35cm) from the bottom edge, herringbone stitch (see p.19) from bottom to top along the whole length of the long edge. On the selvage, stitch through the two layers of interlining and the main fabric; below the fold, only stitch through the interlining. Ideally, use matching thread, but contrast thread will not show on the right side.

5 Fold over the main fabric and the interlining by 2¾in (7cm) at the bottom edge of the curtain. If the interlining moves, use a ruler to tuck it back in place.

6 Turn the two fabrics over again by 2¾in (7cm) to form a double hem.

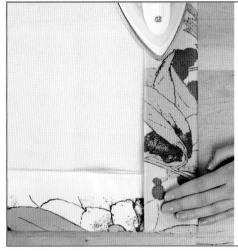

7 Press the hem, pressing the corner especially sharply. Since it is best to press the hem without disturbing the curtain, bring the iron to the curtain and protect the surface underneath with a towel or some folded fabric if required. Repeat Steps 2–7 for the other curtain.

Creating a true miter at the corners

1 Mark the corner with a pin.

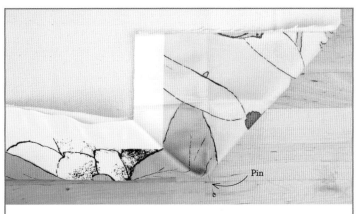

Pin

2 Unfold both fabrics at the corner, then bring the tips of both fabrics back toward the body of the curtain until the pin is at the corner, as shown.

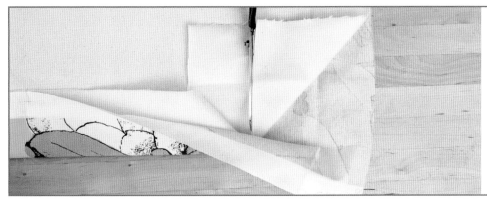

3 Unfold the main fabric. Cut the interlining along the fold from the raw edge toward the pin, as shown.

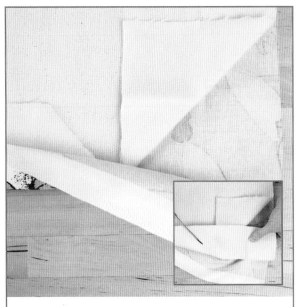

4 Now cut the interlining inside the return at a 45-degree angle to remove some of the excess fabric.

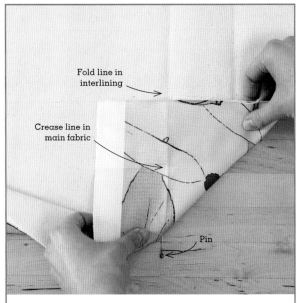

Fold line in interlining

Crease line in main fabric

Pin

5 Fold the main fabric back again so the pin is once more at the corner. To check that everything is straight, the crease line in the main fabric should lie on top of the fold line in the interlining.

6 Cut a muslin rectangle to fit around the drapery weight. Fold and stitch around two sides to form a small pouch. Slip in the weight and sew closed. Place the drapery weight on the main fabric in the return but above the hemline. Stitch in place, taking care not to stitch through to the main fabric.

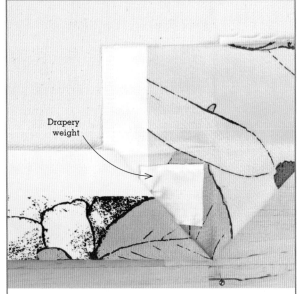

Drapery weight

7 Fold the return back over the weight to create the first 45-degree angle of the miter.

8 Fold the double hem along the first pressed line.

9 Fold the double hem along the second pressed line. The hem and the side will meet at the second 45-degree angle, hiding the weight and creating a true miter.

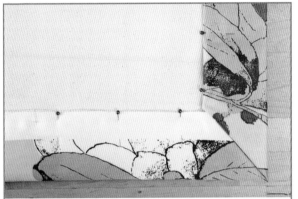

10 Pin partway along the hem and the return to secure the miter. Repeat Steps 1–9 at the other bottom corner. Pin along the other return and the remainder of the hem.

11 Invisible stitch (see p.19) the mitered corners closed.

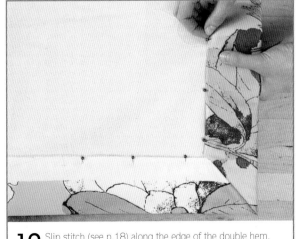

12 Slip stitch (see p.18) along the edge of the double hem. Repeat Steps 1–12 on the other curtain.

Making the lining

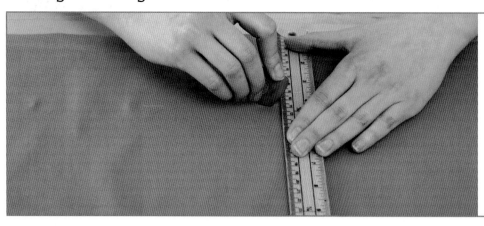

1 Measure and mark a line 4in (10cm) from the bottom of the lining.

2 Turn up the bottom raw edge to meet the line.

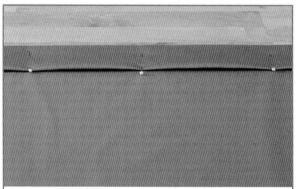

3 Turn up the hem again to create a double hem. Secure with pins.

4 Fold the lining in an accordion fold to make it easier to manage, leaving the pinned hem accessible.

5 Accordion fold the curtain the other way, again leaving the pinned hem accessible.

6 Stitch the hem as close to the fold as possible, unfolding the accordion fold as you go. Keep your fabric as flat and neat as possible.

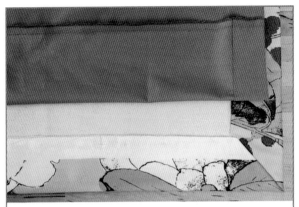

7 Lay the lining on top of the curtain, wrong sides together, aligning the stitching lines of the two hems.

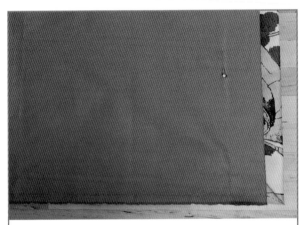

8 Making sure the long sides are also aligned, place a couple of pins along the aligned stitching lines to hold the lining in place. Smooth out the lining.

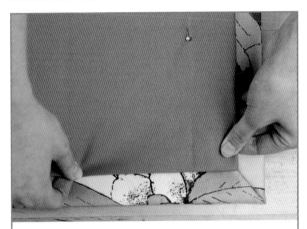

9 Starting at the bottom hem, turn under the long raw edge of the lining to meet the miter.

10 Turn under the rest of the raw edge from hem to top by the same amount. Pin in place.

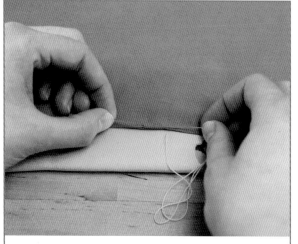

11 Stitch the lining to the curtain by making a few tight slip stitches (see p.18) at the hem end. Continue with an invisible stitch (see p.19) all the way up the long side.

12 Double-check the final length of the curtain. Starting at the hem, measure and mark this length at various points along the width of the curtain.

13 Fold over the top—the main interlined fabric and the lining—at the marks and press.

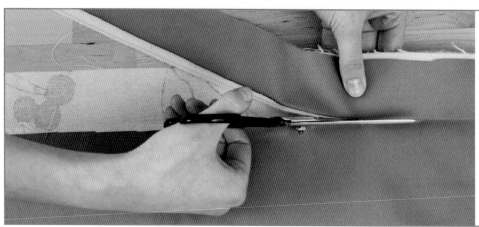

14 Unfold the fabrics, then cut the lining and interlining along the fold line. Fold the main fabric back over the lining.

Attaching the header tape

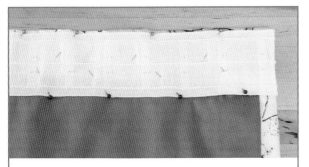

1 Cut the header tape the width of the curtain plus 2⅜in (6cm). Knot the cords at one end of the tape on the wrong side. With the tape face up, place it close to the top edge of the curtain. Turn the knotted end of the tape under and pin in place. At the other end, free the cords from the tape until you can turn under the end to meet the other edge of the curtain. Pin along the top and bottom edges of the tape.

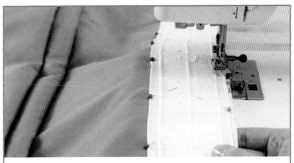

2 Accordion fold the fabric as before. Using a bobbin thread that matches your main fabric and a cream or white top thread, stitch the header tape along a short edge, then pivot and stitch along a long edge, through all the layers. Stitch along the other long edge, then pivot to stitch the other short edge. Sew both long edges in the same direction to prevent puckering.

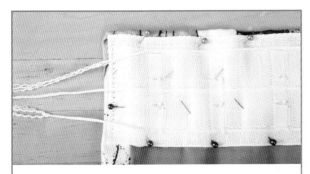

3 Be careful not to sew over the loose ends of the cords. Remove the pins.

4 Pull the cords on the header tape to create pleats, adjusting the curtain so it is half the width of your curtain pole. Secure the cords with a knot. Even out the pleats.

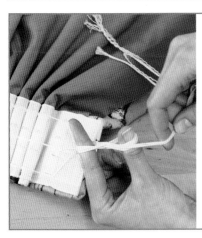

5 Create a figure-eight with the end of the cord.

6 Tuck the figure-eight under the knot to keep it out of the way. Insert curtain hooks into the header tape and hang the curtain. Repeat Steps 1–6 to attach header tape to the other curtain.

SHADES

Making shades

Shades are a simple alternative to curtains for dressing a window. They use far less fabric and give a totally different effect. There are many options when choosing shades, from the system they use for raising and lowering the shade, to the overall look they create.

Measuring

How you measure your window for a shade is determined by whether the shade is to be fixed inside or outside the window recess. A shade inside the recess is usually fixed to the top of the window frame or to the top of the recess. When measuring for a shade fixed outside the recess, first decide where the shade will be hung from. This will be the starting point for the drop measurement. The width is determined by adding 4in (10cm) to the total window width.

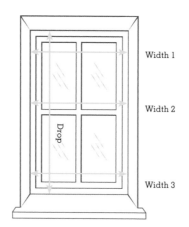

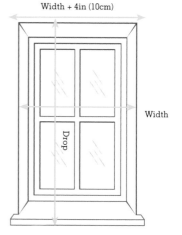

Inside the window recess
Measure the width of the recess at three points. Subtract ⅜in (1cm) from the smallest measurement to get the finished width. This ensures that the shade has room to move up and down. For the drop, measure from the inside fixing point to the windowsill.

Outside the window recess
For the width, measure the width of the recess and add 4in (10cm) to give a 2in (5cm) overlap on each side. This prevents light from coming in at the sides of the lowered shade. For the drop, measure from the fixing point to just below the windowsill.

Raising and lowering shades

What sets different styles of shades apart from each other is how they are raised and lowered. Some shades require you to purchase a special kit to do the job, while other raising and lowering systems can be made using simple materials.

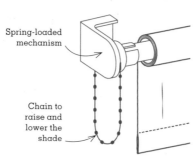

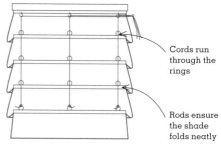

Roller shade
This is made from a kit consisting of a pole, batten, and end brackets. The brackets have a mechanism that is operated when you raise or lower the shade.

Spring-loaded mechanism

Chain to raise and lower the shade

Roman shade
This operates using a pulley system of cords, rods, and rings attached to the back of the shade. The fabric stacks neatly as the shade is opened. Follow the project instructions on pp.172–183 to create the pulley system for your Roman shade.

Cords run through the rings

Rods ensure the shade folds neatly

Types of shades

Some shades lie flat when lowered, and some gather up into soft folds or crisp pleats. Choose a shade according to the look you want and the way you plan to use the shade.

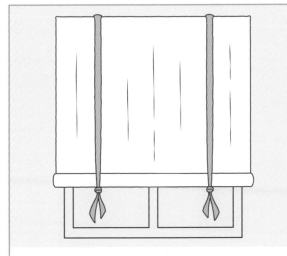

TIE SHADE

This is the simplest type of shade to make at home. It consists of a panel of fabric that is rolled up and unrolled by tightening and loosening a pair of ties. This shade is best in a situation where it can be left at the same drop length most of the time.

LONDON SHADE

The more casual London shade is made like a Roman shade but with no lath at the bottom and without any rods. The result is a shade that gathers into soft folds when it is raised.

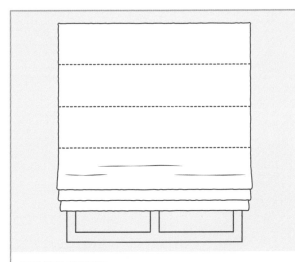

ROMAN SHADE

With its lath at the bottom and rods along its length, a Roman shade stacks into neat pleats as it is raised via its pulley system. It sits well both outside a window recess or inside, giving a crisp, tailored look to a room.

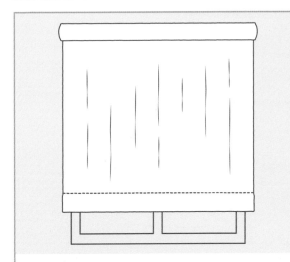

ROLLER SHADE

Roller shades are made using a kit that automatically rolls a stiffened length of fabric around a pole. They have a simple look that is perfect for a bathroom or kitchen.

Tie shade

With its contrasting lining and grosgrain ribbon ties, this roll-up shade looks fresh and pretty, and it is really easy to make. Our professional technique for attaching the Velcro tape at the top of the shade ensures that no stitches will be visible on the right side.

YOU WILL NEED

MATERIALS
- Main fabric
- Interfacing
- Lining fabric
- Velcro fastening tape
- Thread
- Ribbon
- Wooden batten

TOOLS
- Scissors
- Triangle (optional)
- Pins
- Iron and ironing board
- Yardstick
- Pencil
- Staple gun

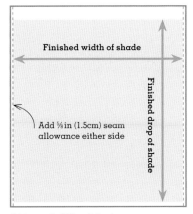

Finished width of shade

Finished drop of shade

Add ⅝in (1.5cm) seam allowance either side

Add a total of 2⅝in (6.5cm) to the overall length

CUTTING MEASUREMENTS

Measure your window (see p.156). Add ⅝in (1.5cm) seam allowance to either side of your shade measurement. Add 2⅝in (6.5cm) to the overall drop for a 2in (5cm) turnover at the top and a ⅝in (1.5cm) seam allowance.

Cutting your fabric

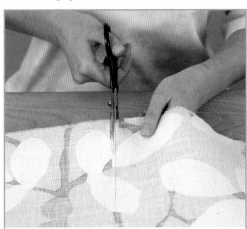

Cut the main fabric, lining, and interfacing to the required size. Check that any pattern in the fabric is centered on each piece and ensure that all the pieces are exactly the same size and are cut at right angles. Use a triangle if necessary.

Assembling the shade

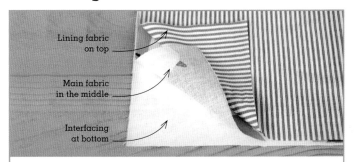

Lining fabric on top

Main fabric in the middle

Interfacing at bottom

1 To assemble your shade, lay the interfacing on the table. Lay the main fabric right side up on top of it, followed by the lining, right side down. Make sure all three fabrics are perfectly aligned, then pin together along both vertical sides.

2 Leaving a ⅝in (1.5cm) seam allowance, stitch both vertical sides together from top to bottom, backstitching at the start and finish of each seam to secure your stitching.

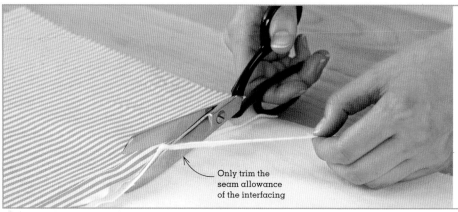

Only trim the seam allowance of the interfacing

3 Lay the tube-shaped shade flat on the ironing board and press the seams open. Make sure when you lay out the shade that all three layers of fabric are flat and you do not iron any wrinkles into the shade. Lay the shade flat on your work surface and trim the seam allowance of the interfacing to ³⁄₁₆ in (5mm).

Cut the bottom corners, cutting through just the seam allowance

4 With the shade flat and the side seams lying flat, pin together the bottom edge. Stitch the edge, leaving a ⅝ in (1.5cm) seam allowance. Trim off the corners to reduce bulk but make sure you do not cut through your stitches. Turn the shade to the right side.

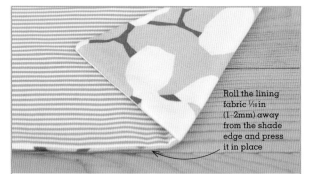

Roll the lining fabric ¹⁄₁₆ in (1–2mm) away from the shade edge and press it in place

5 Place the shade right side down and press along the stitched edges, rolling the lining ¹⁄₁₆ in (1–2mm) away from the main fabric as you go. Turn the shade right side up and smooth out the layers, running your hand from the bottom of the shade to the top.

Making the heading

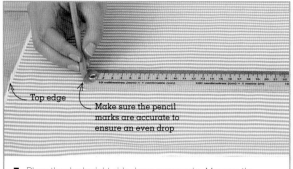

Top edge

Make sure the pencil marks are accurate to ensure an even drop

1 Place the shade right side down once again. Measure the desired length/drop at various points from the bottom edge, marking the fabric at intervals along its width with a pencil or tailor's chalk.

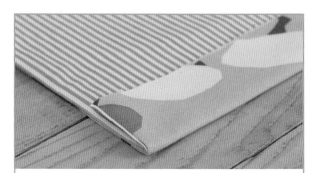

2 Fold over the top of the shade, lining to lining, along the marks. Press to form a crease. This fold will be for attaching the Velcro tape.

Attaching the ties and finishing

1 To determine the length of the ribbon ties, multiply the length of the shade by two and cut two pieces of ribbon to this size. Fold each tie in half and place a pin on the fold. Position each tie with its pin on the fold at the top of the shade and with half the ribbon on the lining side and half on the main fabric side.

2 The ties should be an equal distance from each edge of the shade. Be guided by the way it looks. Pin the ties in place.

Fold

Raw edge

3 With the front of the shade face up, open out the top fold and the ties. Remove the pins and lay a looped strip of Velcro tape with one edge along the fold and the other toward the raw edge. Pin in place, also pinning through the ribbon. Stitch along each of the Velcro tape's two long edges, starting each seam from the same edge of the shade. Catch the ties in the seam as you go and backstitch at the start and finish.

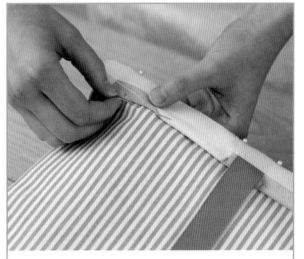

4 Refold the top fold along the Velcro tape, then fold the raw edge under ⅝in (1.5cm). Pin then slip stitch in place. Take care that your stitches do not show on the front of the shade. Use a staple gun to attach the hooked side of the Velcro strip to a wooden batten the width of the blind. Attach the batten to the wall and hang your shade using the Velcro. Roll up the bottom edge and tie with the ribbons.

London shade

This dainty London shade creates an attractive focal point at any window. We have added additional fabric to the length to give the shade extra fullness. Normally left partway down, once its gentle folds have been arranged to best effect it can also be unrolled for privacy.

YOU WILL NEED

MATERIALS
- Main fabric
- Lining fabric
- Hooked self-adhesive Velcro tape and looped sewing Velcro tape (to fit the finished width of the blind)
- Matching thread
- Shade cord
- Rings
- Screw eyes
- Wooden batten

TOOLS
- Measuring tape
- Tailor's chalk
- Scissors
- Pins
- Sewing machine
- Iron
- Tape measure
- Hand sewing needle
- Staple gun
- Bradawl

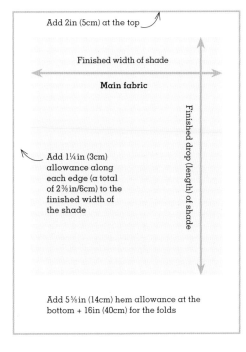

Add 2in (5cm) at the top

Finished width of shade

Main fabric

Add 1¼in (3cm) allowance along each edge (a total of 2⅜in/6cm) to the finished width of the shade

Finished drop (length) of shade

Add 5⅝in (14cm) hem allowance at the bottom + 16in (40cm) for the folds

CUTTING MEASUREMENTS

Decide whether the shade will sit inside or outside the window and measure accordingly (see p.156). Then calculate the cutting measurements for fabric and lining as below:

Main fabric
Width: Finished width of shade + 2⅜in (6cm)
Length: Finished drop (length) of shade + 5⅝in (14cm) for hem + 2in (5cm) for top + 16in (40cm) for decorative folds

Lining
Width: Finished width of shade
Length: As for main fabric

Joining main fabric and lining

1 Square off the fabric (see p.15). Measure your window and cut the main fabric and lining to the dimensions (see above). The lining will be 2⅜in (6cm) narrower than the main fabric.

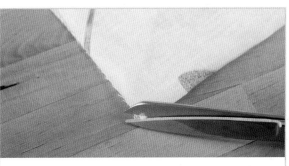

2 Fold both the main fabric and the lining in half lengthwise and mark the center points with a pin or clip with scissors.

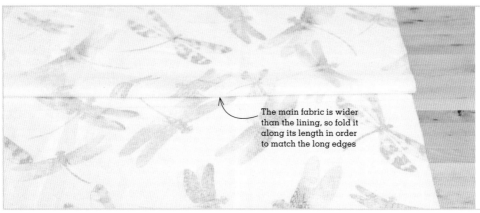

3 Place the lining and the main fabric, right sides together, matching along one long edge. Pin in place. Bring the other long edges together and pin.

The main fabric is wider than the lining, so fold it along its length in order to match the long edges

4 Machine stitch with a ⅝in (1.5cm) seam allowance from top to bottom along each edge.

5 You now have a fabric tube. With the tube wrong side out, maneuver it so that the seams are not at the edges. Press each seam toward the lining along each long edge.

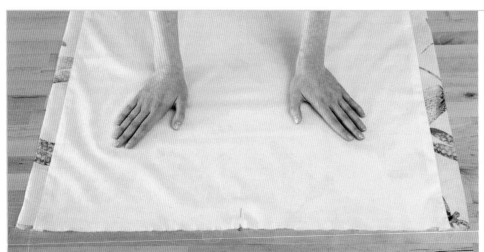

6 Turn the fabric tube right side out and, with the lining facing up, match the center points of the main fabric and the lining top and bottom. Since the lining is narrower than the main fabric, the main fabric will roll inward, forming a return along each edge. Smooth out any wrinkles in the lining.

Making the hem

1 Align the raw edges of the lining and the main fabric at the bottom and pin. Baste together ⅜in (1cm) from the raw edges.

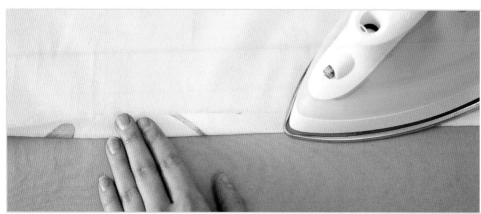

2 With the lining face up, fold over the lining and the main fabric to make a ⅝in (1.5cm) hem along the bottom. Press.

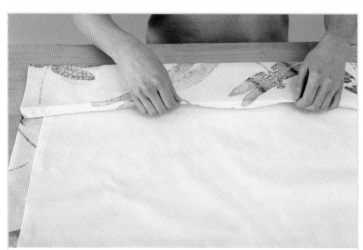

3 Turn the folded fabric a second time to make a hem 4¾in (12cm) deep.

4 Pin, then slip stitch (see p.18) in place along the fold, taking care not to stitch right through to the main fabric.

Making the top

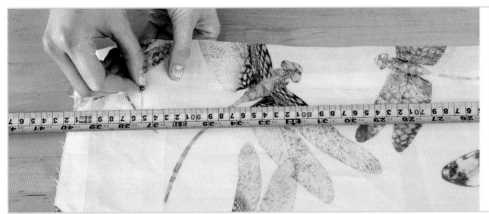

1 With the shade face down, measure the desired drop at various points from the bottom edge, marking the fabric at intervals along its width, across the top, with a row of pins. Fold the fabric along the pins toward the wrong side and press.

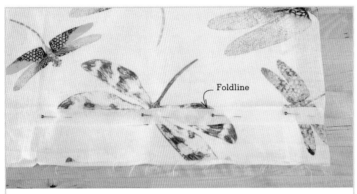

Foldline

2 Remove the pins, open out the fabric, and with the shade lining side down, lay a strip of looped sewing Velcro tape with one edge along the fold line and the other toward the raw edge. Pin in place.

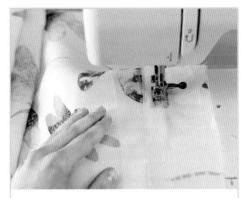

3 Stitch along each of the two long edges of the Velcro tape, sewing in the same direction each time.

4 With the shade face down, fold over the fabric right along the edge of the Velcro tape, as shown. Fold the raw edge under and pin.

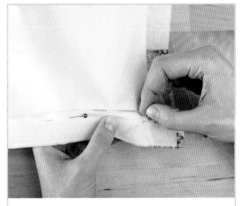

5 Slip stitch the hem in place along the fold. Take care not to stitch through to the front layer.

Attaching the rings

1 To position the first ring, with the shade face down, measure 2⅜ in (6cm) from the bottom edge of the shade and 3¼ in (8cm) from the side. Mark this point with crossed pins.

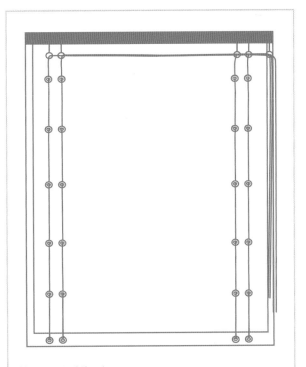

Placement of the rings
The rings are stitched on in two sets of two parallel lines.

2 Measure from this point to the top of the shade. Divide this measurement by the number of folds you require. For a shade around 52in (130cm), you will need 6, 7, or 8 folds, depending on which number divides most accurately into your previous measurement. Once you have found the number, measure the positions of that number of rings accordingly and mark with a line of crossed pins from bottom to top.

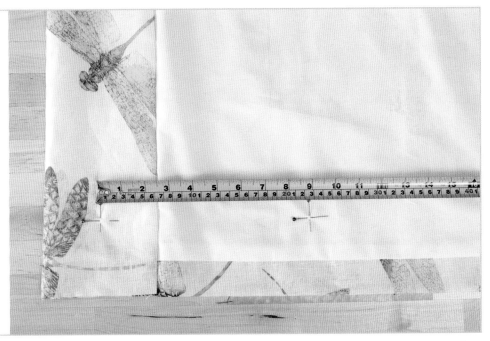

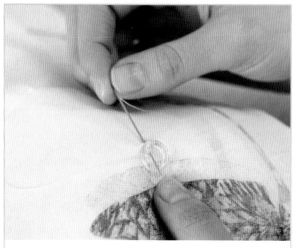

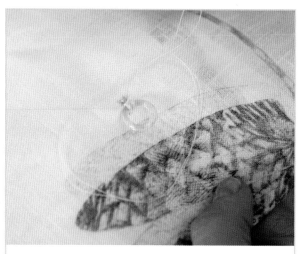

3 To attach the first ring, knot the thread in your needle and sew through the fabric at the crossed pins. Holding the ring in place, take a few stitches through it.

4 To finish, wrap the thread around the ring and take the needle through the loop to tighten the thread.

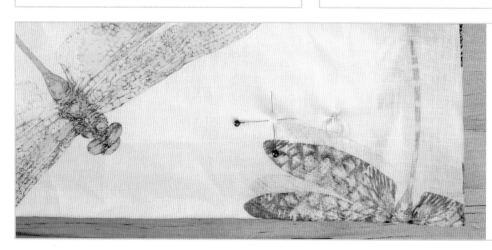

5 Repeat to sew one ring at each pair of crossed pins in the same way, ensuring that they are all parallel to the side of the shade. Pin a second line of crossed pins 1 ⅝in (4cm) in from the first. Sew a second line of rings at the pins in the same way.

6 Constantly checking that the lines all align vertically and horizontally, measure, mark, and sew on two lines of rings at the other side of the shade in exactly the same way.

Preparing the batten

1 Cut a piece of muslin longer than the batten and wide enough to wrap around it with some overlap. Staple the muslin to the batten along one long edge.

2 Wrap the muslin neatly around the batten and staple in place. Trim off any excess muslin.

3 Fold the ends together neatly over the batten. Staple in place then trim off any excess muslin.

4 Peel the backing off a length of hooked self-adhesive Velcro tape, stick it to one wide face of the batten, then staple at intervals to secure.

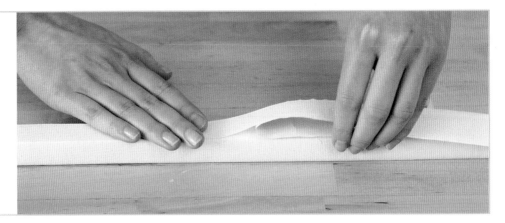

5 Turn the batten so that a face that is adjacent to the Velcro tape is facing you. Use a bradawl to make a hole 3 ¼ in (8cm) from the end of the batten and a second hole 4 ¾ in (12cm) from the end.

6 Insert screw eyes into the holes. Repeat at the same distances from the other end of the batten.

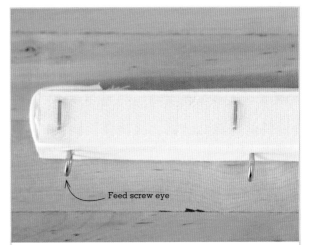

Feed screw eye

7 Decide at which side of the shade you would like the pull cord to be and add one more screw eye—the feed screw eye—about ⅜ in (1cm) from the end, on that side.

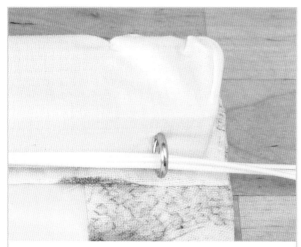

8 Cut four lengths of cord, each the length of the shade, plus the length of the batten, plus another two-thirds the length of the shade. Tie the end of each cord to the bottom ring in each row, then thread it through the other rings in the row and through the screw eye at the top. Pass each cord through all the screw eyes to its right or left toward the feed screw eye. Check that the shade gathers correctly, then unthread the cords and remove the shade from the batten.

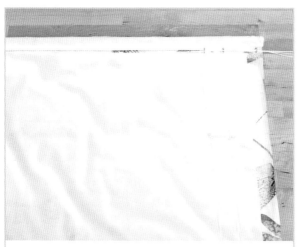

9 Attach the batten to the window frame with the Velcro tape facing out, reattach the shade, and rethread the cords through the screw eyes. Check that the shade hangs evenly and correct the shade cords if necessary. Gather the ends of the cords together and tie in a knot. Attach the cleat to the wall or window frame. It must be no lower than 60in (150cm) from the floor to prevent children from tangling themselves in the cords. Wrap the cords around the cleat and shape the folds to your liking.

Attach a cleat to the window frame, and use to keep the cord from slipping. Just wind the cord around a few times to secure.

Roman shade

With its pleats supported by rods concealed in pockets at the back, a Roman shade is a neat, tailored solution for a window treatment. This project is fairly complex but the complexity lies in calculating the measurements for the pleats, so you need to hone your math skills. The sewing is a breeze.

YOU WILL NEED

MATERIALS

- Main fabric (see right for quantity)
- Lining fabric
- Matching thread
- Wooden lath, cut to the width of the blind
- Roman shade rods
- Roman shade rings
- Shade cord
- Screw eyes
- Hooked self-adhesive Velcro tape and looped sewing Velcro tape

TOOLS

- Triangle (optional)
- Measuring tape
- Tailor's chalk
- Scissors
- Pins
- Iron
- Sewing machine
- Yardstick
- Staple gun
- Bradawl

CUTTING MEASUREMENTS

Decide whether the shade will sit inside or outside the window and measure accordingly (see p.156). Then calculate the cutting measurements for fabric and lining as below:

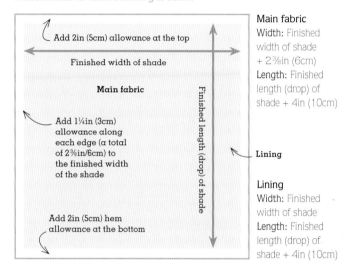

Add 2in (5cm) allowance at the top

Finished width of shade

Main fabric

Finished length (drop) of shade

Add 1¼in (3cm) allowance along each edge (a total of 2⅜in/6cm) to the finished width of the shade

Add 2in (5cm) hem allowance at the bottom

Lining

Main fabric
Width: Finished width of shade + 2⅜in (6cm)
Length: Finished length (drop) of shade + 4in (10cm)

Lining
Width: Finished width of shade + 2⅜in (6cm)
Length: Finished length (drop) of shade + 4in (10cm)

Cutting the fabric

Lay the main fabric on the work surface right side up. Square off the bottom (see p.15) and cut off the excess. Measure, mark, and cut the fabric following the instructions above.

Joining fabric and lining

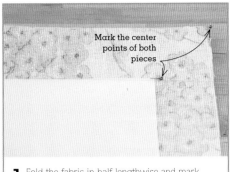

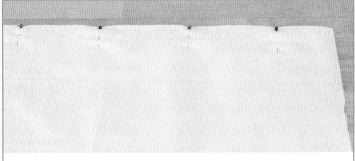

1 Fold the fabric in half lengthwise and mark the center points top and bottom with pins. Square off the lining, as before, and cut to the desired width. Mark the center points top and bottom, as before.

2 Lay the fabric and lining right side to right side. Match the bottom edge and one side edge. Pin together along the side edge, making sure the raw edges remain aligned.

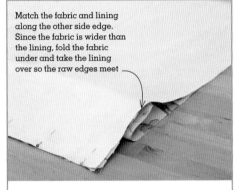

3 Pin together, then machine stitch along both side edges from top to bottom with a ⅝in (1.5cm) seam allowance. The shade and lining now form a tube.

4 Lay the tube on the ironing board. Maneuver the seams so that they are not at the edges of the tube, then press both seam allowances toward the main fabric along both seams. This will encourage the seam allowances to lie flat when the shade is turned to the right side.

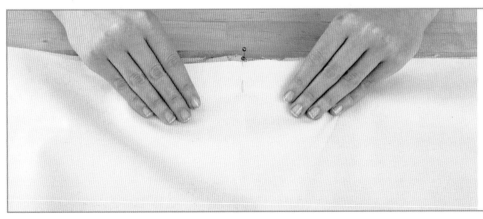

5 Turn the shade right side out and with the main fabric face down, match the center points of the main fabric and the lining, top and bottom.

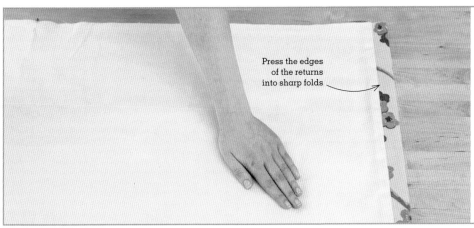

Press the edges of the returns into sharp folds

6 Smooth out the shade from the center to the edges. Equal ⅝in (1.5cm) returns of the main fabric should now be visible along each edge and the seam allowances should lie flat under the returns.

Preparing for the lath

1 With the shade face down, fold over ⅝in (1.5cm) along the bottom edge.

2 Fold over another 1⅜in (3.5cm) to make a hem. Press.

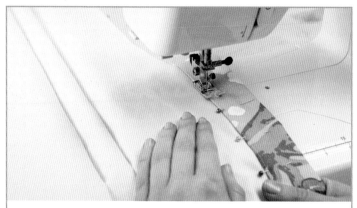

3 Pin the corners of the hem in place first, ensuring they do not overhang the edge of the shade. Then pin along the hem, taking in any excess.

4 Using a medium-length stitch, bobbin thread to match the main fabric, and with the needle to the left to allow you to stitch as close to the edge as possible, machine stitch along the folded edge. Press to set the stitches. This is the channel for the lath at the bottom of the shade.

Attaching the Velcro tape

1 With the shade face down, measure the finished length up from the bottom edge at several points across the width. Mark with a row of pins.

2 Turn the fabric over along the pinned line. Press, then draw a line ¾in (2cm) from the folded edge. Cut along the line.

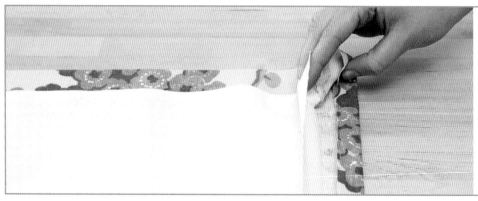

3 Unfold the fabric and separate the main fabric and the lining. Refold the main fabric along the fold line.

4 Fold the fabric around the corner of the shade, then fold the corner back into place.

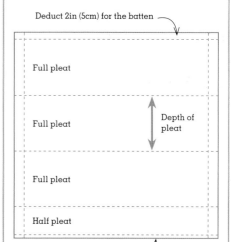

5 Fold the edge of the lining under so it sits ³⁄₁₆in (5mm) below the top edge of the shade. Press.

Sew the Velcro tape in the same direction along both edges to prevent the fabric from twisting

6 Cut a length of looped Velcro tape to the width of the shade. Position the Velcro tape along the top edge of the shade, approximately ¹⁄₈in (3mm) down from the edge. Pin, then machine stitch the Velcro tape in place along both long edges.

Calculating the pleats

- A Roman shade has a half pleat at the bottom and a number of full pleats. The half pleat is made a little deeper so that when the shade is up the half pleat extends farther than the folded pleats.
- For shades up to 60in (150cm) long, the optimal depth of each full pleat is 8–12in (20–30cm). For longer shades, the best depth is 12–16in (30–40cm).
- Start by measuring the length of the shade from top to bottom. Deduct 2in (5cm), which is the depth of the batten, then deduct another ³⁄₈in (1cm), which is the extra length you need for the half pleat.

Deduct 2in (5cm) for the batten

Full pleat	
Full pleat	Depth of pleat
Full pleat	
Half pleat	

Deduct ³⁄₈in (1cm) to allow extra length to half pleat

- After making the deductions, divide the remaining amount by 3.5, 4.5, 5.5, or 6.5, depending on which of these calculations results in the optimum pleat size.
- Round the resulting number up or down to the nearest quarter inch (half centimeter).
- To calculate the depth of the half pleat, divide the measurement of a full pleat in two. Add the ³⁄₈in (1cm) deducted at the beginning and add any excess you rounded off from the full pleats.

Marking the pleats

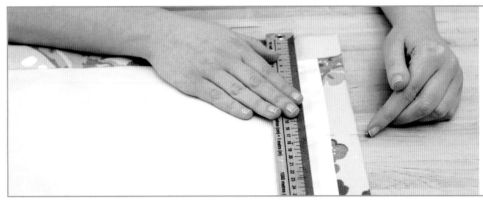

1 Calculate the measurements for the pleats (see p.177). With the shade face down and starting from the hem, measure the depth of the half pleat along one return and mark it with a pin. Mark in the same way along the other return.

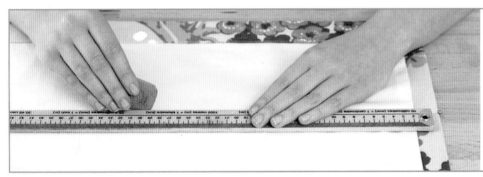

2 Check your measurements to ensure they are correct and equal on both sides. Then, using the yardstick, draw a very faint chalk line across the shade from pin to pin.

3 Measure the depth of the first full pleat from the first line and lightly mark. Again, check your measurements and mark with pins as before.

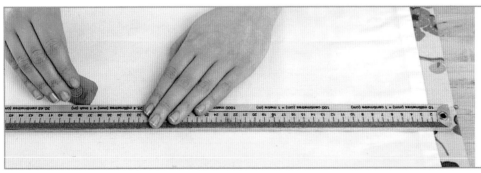

4 Lightly draw a line to join the second pair of pins. Repeat Steps 3–4 to mark the positions of all the pleats.

Preparing for the rods

1 Cut strips of lining fabric 3⅝in (9cm) deep and the finished width of the shade. Fold each strip in half lengthwise, then press. Open them out again.

2 Fold the raw edges into the center fold and press again.

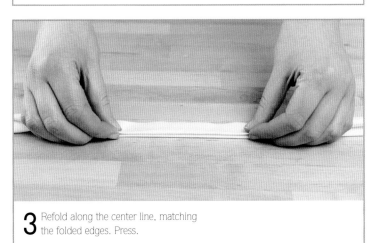

3 Refold along the center line, matching the folded edges. Press.

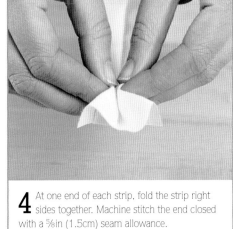

4 At one end of each strip, fold the strip right sides together. Machine stitch the end closed with ⅝in (1.5cm) seam allowance.

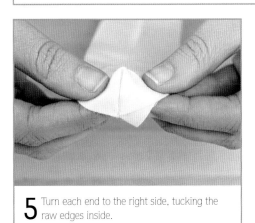

5 Turn each end to the right side, tucking the raw edges inside.

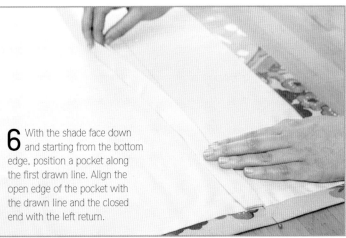

6 With the shade face down and starting from the bottom edge, position a pocket along the first drawn line. Align the open edge of the pocket with the drawn line and the closed end with the left return.

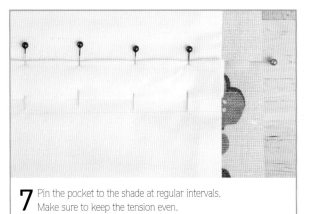

7 Pin the pocket to the shade at regular intervals. Make sure to keep the tension even.

8 To neaten the open end of the pocket, first open out the pocket fold. Then turn the raw edge back toward the pocket so that the folded edge is level with the lining.

9 Fold the end of the pocket back into place and secure with a pin.

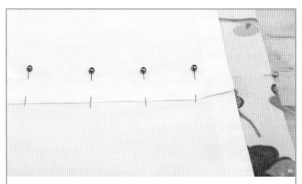

10 Pin on the remaining pockets in the same way.

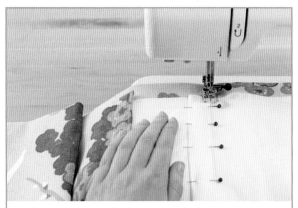

11 Using bobbin thread that matches the main fabric and upper thread that matches the lining, machine stitch the first pocket in place as close to the pinned folded edge as possible. Adjust the position of the needle if necessary to allow you to stitch closer to the edge.

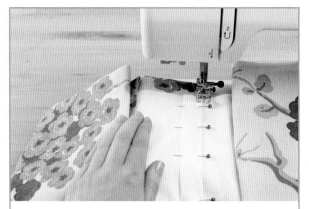

12 Machine stitch the remaining pockets in place, folding the shade under the arm of the machine as you go. You now have a pocket for each rod.

Assembling the shade

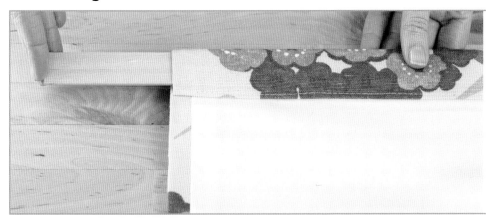

1 Insert the wooden lath inside the channel at the bottom edge. Slip stitch (see p.18) both ends of the channel closed.

2 Cut the required number of rods ⅜in (1cm) shorter than the pockets. Slip the rods in the pockets and slip stitch the open end of each pocket closed.

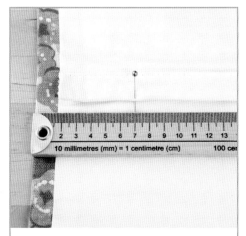

3 With the shade face down, measure 2¾in (7cm) along the first pocket from the edge of the shade. Mark with a pin. Repeat for both ends of all the pockets.

4 Knot the thread in your needle and sew through the fabric from back to front at the first pin. Holding the ring in place, take a stitch through the front of the ring and back through the fabric. Repeat a few times. To finish, wrap the thread around the ring and take the needle through the loop in the thread to secure. Repeat to attach a ring at the other pins.

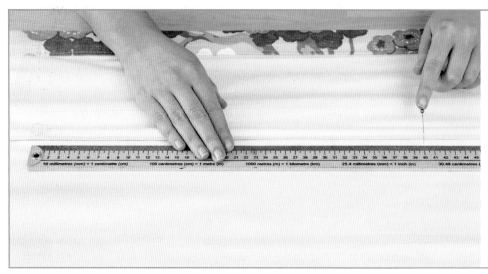

5 Mark the position of the rest of the rings along the first pocket between the rings at either end, first spacing them out by eye. Measure to ensure they are evenly spaced and no more than 16in (40cm) apart. Mark the position of each with a pin, then stitch on the rings at the pins as above. Sew rings to the other pockets, aligning them vertically.

Preparing the batten

1 Cover the batten with muslin or cotton batiste and attach a length of hooked Velcro tape (see pp.169–170, Steps 1–4). Turn the batten so that a face that is adjacent to the Velcro tape is facing you. Use a bradawl to make a hole 2¾in (7cm) from each end. Insert a screw eye.

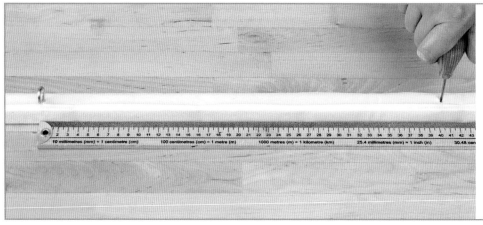

2 Measure the horizontal distance between the rings on the shade and using these measurements, insert the remaining screw eyes in the batten.

Feed screw eye

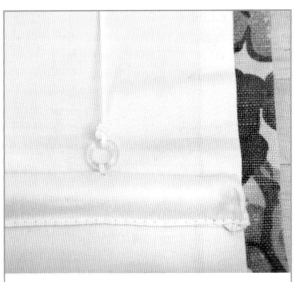

3 Decide at which side of the shade you would like the pull cord to be. With the Velcro tape facing away from you, add one more screw eye—the feed screw eye—between the end of the batten and the first screw eye on that side.

4 Calculate how much shade cord is needed by adding the length of the shade to the width plus 40in (1m). Cut one length for each line of rings. Attach a length of cord to each bottom ring, knotting it tightly.

5 Thread the cord through the other rings in the row and through the feed screw eye at the top. Pass each cord through all the screw eyes to its right or left toward the feed screw eye. Check that the shade folds up correctly, then unthread the cords and remove the shade from the batten. Attach the batten to the window frame with the Velcro tape facing out, rethread the cords, and attach the shade with the Velcro tape. Tie the ends of the cords together in a knot. Attach the cleat to the wall or frame, no lower than 60in (150cm) from the floor to prevent children from getting tangled in the cords. Wrap the cords around the cleat.

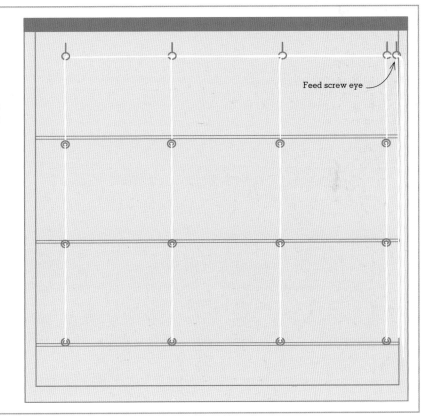

Feed screw eye

Roller shade

A roller shade brings privacy to a room and is a chic, contemporary window treatment that is easy to make, thanks to commercial roller shade kits. Cutting to size, sewing the sides and a hem, stiffening the fabric, and attaching the pole are almost all you need to do for professional results every time.

YOU WILL NEED

MATERIALS
- Fabric
- Matching thread

TOOLS
- Roller shade kit, consisting of pole, batten, and end brackets
- Pins
- Ruler
- Tailor's chalk
- Scissors
- Sewing machine
- Clothesline or shower rod (optional)
- Spray bottle (optional)
- Bucket (optional)
- Hacksaw
- PVA solution

BEFORE YOU START

How you measure for a shade will be determined by whether it is to go inside or outside the window recess. Measure the finished width and drop (see pp.156–157). Following the manufacturer's instructions, cut the pole to the required length. Use the diagram, right, to determine the cutting width and length of your shade.

Cutting length:
Drop of shade + diameter of pole + 2in (5cm) at the top + 2⅜in (6cm) at the bottom for the hem

Cutting width:
Width of pole (excluding end brackets) + ¾in (2cm) seam allowance

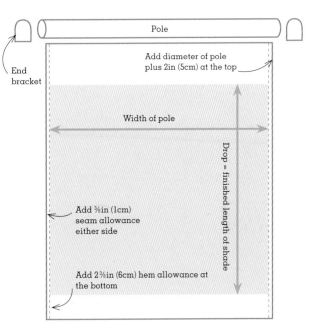

End bracket

Pole

Add diameter of pole plus 2in (5cm) at the top

Width of pole

Drop = finished length of shade

Add ⅜in (1cm) seam allowance either side

Add 2⅜in (6cm) hem allowance at the bottom

Measuring and cutting out

1 Decide which part of the pattern is the center of your shade. Place a pin at the center, then add more pins in a straight line above and below this point.

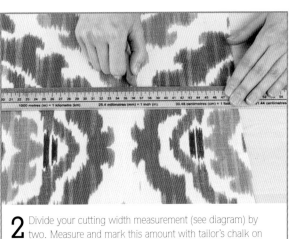

2 Divide your cutting width measurement (see diagram) by two. Measure and mark this amount with tailor's chalk on either side of the row of pins, the length of the fabric.

3 Decide where you would like the top of the shade to be and draw a line here. Measure the cutting length from this line and mark another line. Cut along the marked lines to cut out the shade.

Stitching the sides and hem

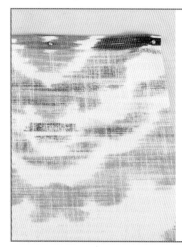

1 With the right side face down, fold over ⅜in (1cm) along each long edge of the shade. Press in place and pin. Since the fabric will be treated with stiffener, it will not fray, so it does not need to be folded twice.

2 Using invisible thread in the bobbin and a medium-length stitch, machine stitch along the folded fabric as close to the raw edge as you can. Sew both edges of the shade from the same direction.

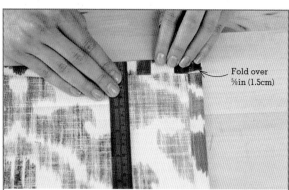

Fold over ⅝in (1.5cm)

3 With the right side still face down, fold over 2⅜in (6cm) along the bottom edge and press. Unfold the fabric, then fold over ⅝in (1.5cm).

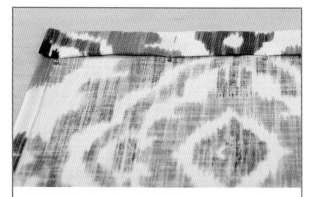

4 Refold the fabric along the 2⅜in (6cm) crease to create a channel, ensuring the sides of the fabric line up neatly. Secure with pins, then machine stitch as close to the first fold as possible. Move the needle to the left if necessary.

Treating with stiffener and assembling

1 Hang the hemmed fabric on a clothesline or shower rod, or ask someone to hold it. Spray with PVA solution and let dry. Alternatively, dip the fabric in a bucket of PVA solution and hang it up to dry.

2 Cut the batten to the finished width of the shade using a hacksaw. When the fabric is dry, insert the batten in the hem.

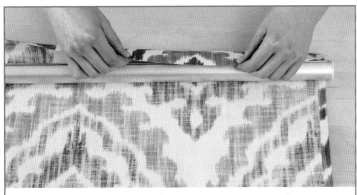

3 Following the manufacturer's instructions, remove the protective layer from the tape on the roller shade pole. Wrap the top, raw edge of the shade around the pole.

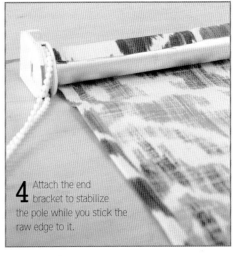

4 Attach the end bracket to stabilize the pole while you stick the raw edge to it.

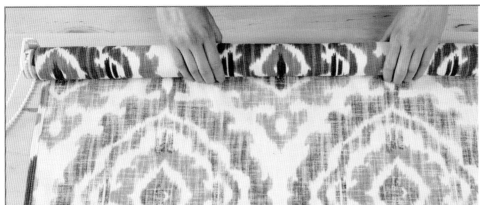

5 Wrap the shade firmly around the pole. Remove the end bracket. Attach the second bracket and mount the shade.

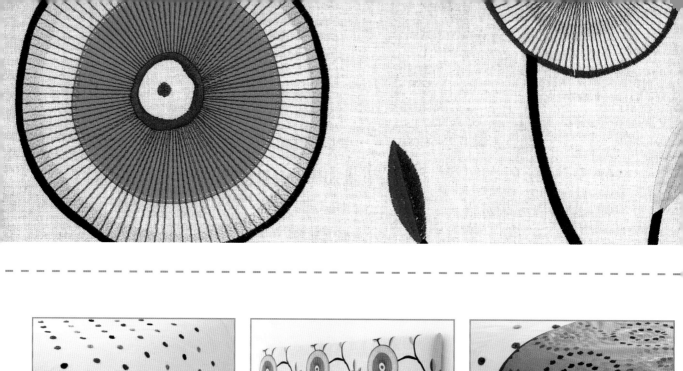

BEDDING

Making bedding

We spend so much time in our bedrooms that they should be spaces we really love. While the right paint and flooring are good starting points, home furnishings can make all the difference between stark surroundings and sumptuous ones. Here we look at some of the lovely bedroom furnishings you can make to give your bedroom the edge.

Dressings for beds

A well-dressed bed makes a bedroom feel luxurious, and having winter and summer sets of bedding is a clever way to freshen up your bedroom from season to season. Failing that, simply changing the decorative touches once in a while will give your bedroom a quick and easy style makeover. For best results, aim to keep the rest of your bedroom's decor neutral.

BEDSPREAD DROP

The drop, or overhang, of a bedspread or bed runner is determined by its purpose and your taste. A generous, floor-length bedspread looks fabulous, but there's no point in having one if you also have a valance. If that's the case, a bedspread that just overhangs the bottom edge of the mattress is a much better choice.

To calculate the finished width of your bedspread, measure the width of the mattress from side to side. Then measure from the top edge of the mattress down, to the length you'd like your bedspread to be. Multiply this drop by two and add it to the width measurement to get the total finished width.

To calculate the total finished length, measure the length of the mattress from top edge to bottom edge. Add just one drop to get the total finished length.

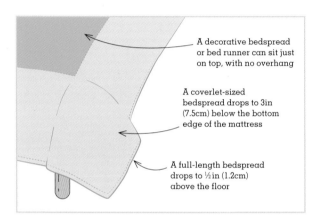

A decorative bedspread or bed runner can sit just on top, with no overhang

A coverlet-sized bedspread drops to 3in (7.5cm) below the bottom edge of the mattress

A full-length bedspread drops to ½in (1.2cm) above the floor

New headboards for old

Have you got a tired old headboard, or have you found an old-fashioned bargain in a secondhand store? If so, re-covering it can give it a new lease on life at minimum cost.

If the headboard padding is in good condition, you can simply re-cover it, either with a fixed cover or a removable slipcover. Whichever type of cover you choose to make, if the padding has worn a bit thin, or your headboard is nothing more than a piece of wood, just add some batting to pad it out and soften its corners.

If you're feeling especially handy, you can make an entirely new headboard using a piece of plywood cut to the size and shape of your choice. This option can then be padded and covered in your fabric, giving you total design freedom.

Lots of layers

Layers are the key to a well-dressed, sumptuous-looking bed. A covered headboard provides a good starting point. As you are unlikely to change its cover frequently, either choose a fabric you love, or go for something neutral. Next come the bedspread and bed runner—although you may not want both. These give another opportunity to add pattern and texture. Finally, add pillows in a variety of decorative fabrics to tie in with your decor and pull the whole look together.

PILLOWS
An array of decorative throw pillows adds texture and color to your bed dressing. For extra interest, try mixing and matching pillows in a few different fabrics and patterns. See pp.22–49 and 58–77 for more information on the variety of pillows you can make.

HEADBOARD
A covered headboard sets the stage for your bed and can look decadent compared to a simple wooden headboard. If you choose a headboard with a slipcover, it's easy to remove it for cleaning or if you want a change of mood.

BEDSPREAD
A bedspread adds yet another layer, and therefore an extra level of luxury, to your bed. Bedspreads can be made to different lengths and in different weights to suit your needs.

BED RUNNER
A bed runner sits across the bed and gives a contemporary, polished look. It is a good way to add a splash of color, texture, or pattern to otherwise plain bedding, and does not require a great deal of fabric.

Light bedspread

Lightweight but firm, thanks to its inner layer of batting held in place by the contrast border, this fresh-looking bedspread is perfect for warm summer nights. We have made our bedspread with finished dimensions of 94½ x 102⅜in (240 x 260cm)—the right size for a queen or double bed.

YOU WILL NEED

MATERIALS
- 16½ft (5m) home decor fabric for front
- 94⅜ x 100¾in (236 x 256cm) sheeting fabric for back
- 94⅜ x 100¾in (236cm x 256cm) batting
- 108in (2.7m) contrast fabric for the border
- Matching thread

TOOLS
- Ruler
- Tailor's chalk
- Triangle (optional)
- Iron
- Scissors
- Pins
- Hand sewing needle
- Sewing machine
- Pencil

For a professional finish, join the panels symmetrically

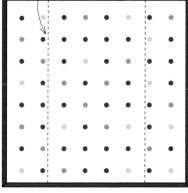

Bedspread front
Home decor fabric is not usually wide enough to make a bedspread for a double bed, so it is made in three panels. Cut the first panel to 100¾in (256cm), then follow the instructions to cut the other two.

Border adds 1⅜in (3.5cm) on all sides

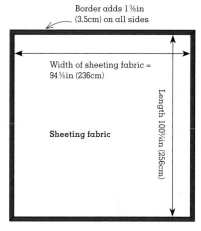

Width of sheeting fabric = 94⅜in (236cm)

Length 100¾in (256cm)

Sheeting fabric

Bedspread back
We have made the back from 94⅜in (236cm) wide sheeting fabric cut to 100¾in (256cm) long. If necessary, you can piece the back from narrower fabric in the same way as the front.

Cutting out the front panels

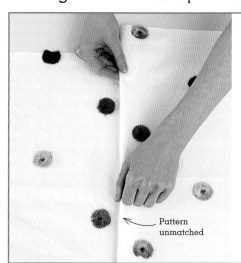

Pattern unmatched

1 Cut the center panel of the bedspread to the required length, in this case 100¾in (256cm), using the full width of the fabric. Lay this on the work surface right side up. Before cutting the two side panels, you must match the pattern. With the right side up, fold under the selvage of the remaining fabric and lay it so its folded edge overlaps the central panel.

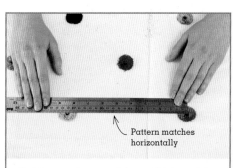

Pattern matches horizontally

2 Maneuver the second piece of fabric until the pattern matches horizontally across the two pieces. Then measure the distance between the horizontal pattern repeat and move the second piece of fabric until this distance also matches across the two pieces.

3 Mark the excess fabric of the second piece at the edge of the fold top and bottom, as shown.

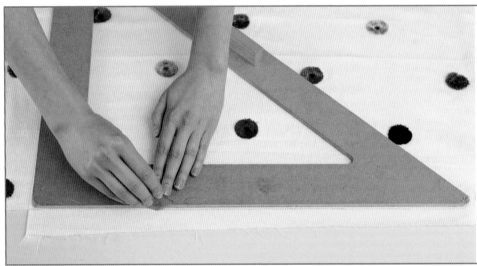

4 Square off (see p.15) the second piece of fabric. Cut off the excess fabric to make this piece the same length as the center panel.

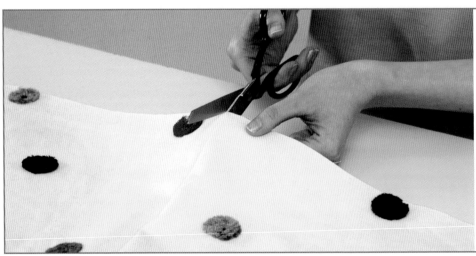

5 Fold the trimmed piece in half lengthwise and press along the fold. Unfold the fabric and cut along the fold to create the two side panels.

Joining the front panels

1 With the center panel right side up, position one of the side panels alongside, selvage to selvage. Fold under the selvage of the side panel. As before, check the horizontal alignment of the pattern across the two pieces, and check that the distance between the pattern repeat is always correct. Pin in place.

2 Slip stitch (see p.18) the two panels together along the folded edge, checking that the pattern matches all the way along. Remove the pins and press on the right side.

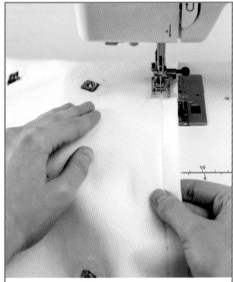

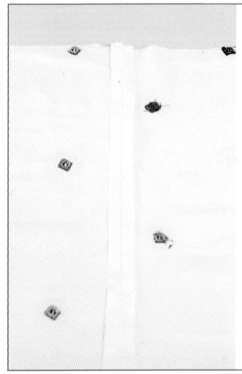

3 Fold back the side panel so that both panels are right sides together and the seam allowance is exposed. Accordion fold the fabric to keep it out of the way and machine stitch along the fold line from top to bottom.

4 Align the second side panel selvage to selvage with the center panel in the same way and machine stitch together as before. Press both seams open. Measure, mark, and cut the joined piece of fabric—the bedspread front—so that it is 94⅜in (236cm) wide.

Joining the layers

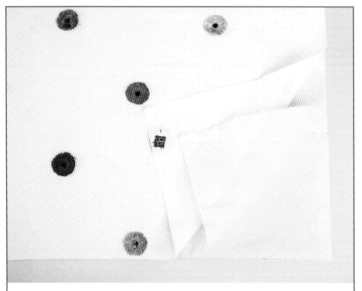

1 Lay the sheeting fabric on the work surface or floor wrong side up. Smooth out any wrinkles. Place the batting on top, then lay the bedspread front on top of that, right side up. Match the raw edges all around. Smooth out any wrinkles.

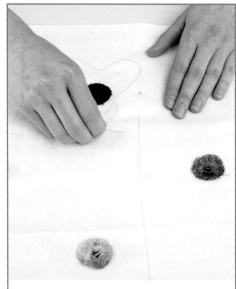

2 Baste the three layers together with horizontal and vertical rows of stitching approximately 8in (20cm) apart.

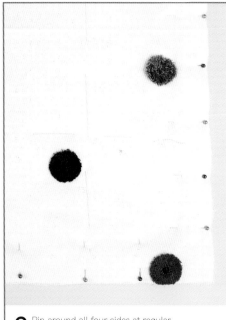

3 Pin around all four sides at regular, close intervals.

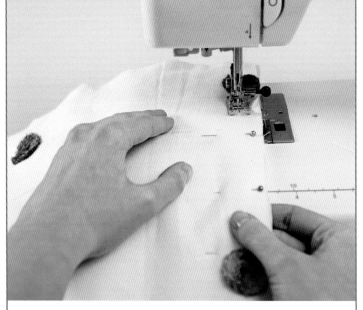

4 Using a large stitch, machine stitch around all four sides within the ⅝in (1.5cm) seam allowance. This will stabilize the edges to allow the border to be attached with ease. Remove the basting stitches.

Making the border

1 The border is folded in half and wraps around the bedspread. It will be mitered at the corners on top and underneath; this is a double miter. For this you must add 2in (5cm) at both ends of each border piece, so cut two pieces, each 96⅞ x 5¼in (246 x 13cm) and two more pieces, each 104¾ x 5¼in (266 x 13cm). With right sides together, press the ends of each piece lengthwise to find the center points.

2 Unfold a 104¾in (266cm) border piece and on the wrong side, draw a ⅜in (1.5cm) seam allowance around each end. Extend the seam allowance lines along the long sides by at least 2¾in (7cm).

3 Measure 2in (5cm) down from each corner and mark the seam allowance lines at these points.

4 Align the ruler between a center point and a 2in (5cm) mark, then join the points with a line. Repeat on the other side of the center point. The resulting 90-degree angle marks the double miters on either end of the longer border pieces.

5 Repeat at both ends of the other 104¾in (266cm) border piece.

6 Place the end of one long border piece right sides together with the end of a short border piece. Secure with pins. Repeat to join another long piece to the free end of the short piece, then join the free end of that long piece to the second short piece. Finish by joining the two free ends to make a rectangle.

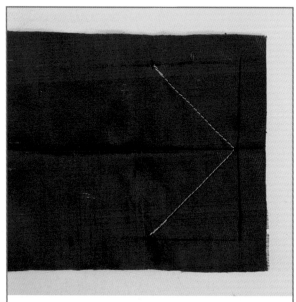

7 Machine stitch the pieces together along the 90-degree angle, pivoting at the point. Backstitch at the beginning and end of the seams to secure them. Make sure that you do not stitch inside the seam allowance.

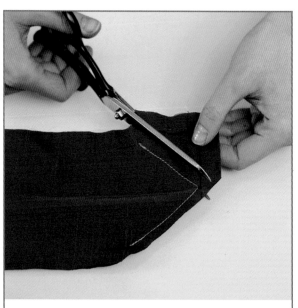

8 Trim off the excess fabric at all four corners of the rectangle, making sure that you do not cut through the stitches.

Attaching the border

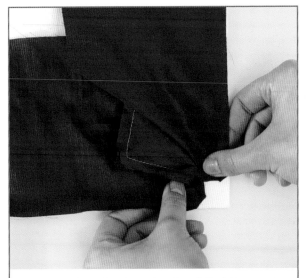

1 Lay the bedspread on the work surface. With right sides together, match the corners of the border with the corners of the bedspread. Open out and fold back the seam allowance at each corner of the border to create a tiny right angle.

2 Pin just the seam allowance of the first corner to the bedspread. Maneuver, or "walk," the border around the bedspread to check that it fits.

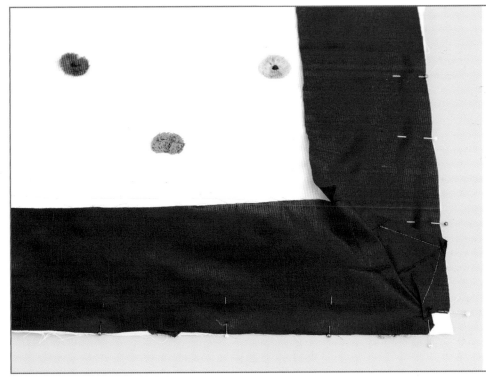

3 Secure the other three corners with pins in the same way, then pin the border to the bedspread along the sides.

4 Machine stitch along one side with a ⅝in (1.5cm) seam allowance. When you reach the first corner, keep the double miter out of the way, lower the needle into the fabric, and raise the presser foot.

5 Pivot the fabric, fold the double miter out of the way to the other side, then lower the foot. Continue around the bedspread, pivoting at the remaining corners in the same way.

6 Lay the bedspread on the work surface face down. Turn the double miters of the border to the right side.

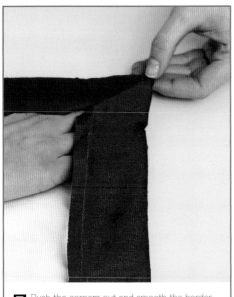

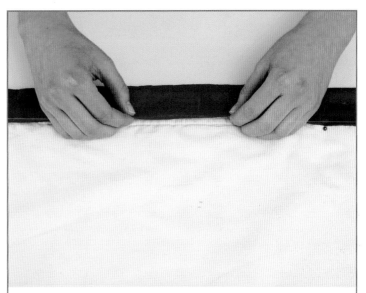

7 Push the corners out and smooth the border flat along the edges of the bedspread.

8 Fold under ⅝in (1.5cm) along the raw edge of the border and pin in place, covering the line of stitching underneath. Slip stitch in place (see p.18) with tight, close stitches no more than ⅜in (1cm) apart. Alternatively, machine stitch in place using a blind hem foot.

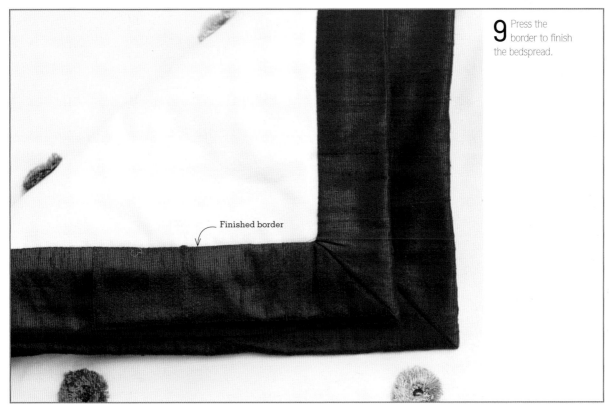

9 Press the border to finish the bedspread.

Finished border

Bed runner

This lightly padded, coordinated bed runner makes the perfect finishing touch when dressing a bed, and it is great for adding an extra layer of coziness around your feet at night, too. Make sure you add borders of the same width at each end so your runner is symmetrical. Our simple instructions show you how.

YOU WILL NEED

MATERIALS
- Main fabric
- Backing fabric
- Fabric in two colors for the borders
- Fabric for the flat piping
- 94½ x 24in (240 x 60cm) cotton batting
- Matching thread

TOOLS
- Scissors
- Pins
- Sewing machine
- Hand sewing needle

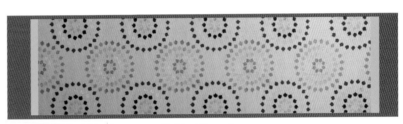

Finished dimensions
94½in (240cm) x 24in (60cm)

CUTTING MEASUREMENTS:

Top: cut 1 rectangle, 81 x 25¼in (206 x 63cm) from main fabric

Backing: cut 1 rectangle, 81 x 25¼in (206 x 63cm) from backing fabric

Narrow border (yellow): cut 2 rectangles, 4 x 25¼in (10 x 63cm)

Wide border (pink): cut 2 rectangles, 12⅜in x 25¼in (31 x 63cm)

Flat piping: cut 2 lengths, each 95½in (243cm) by 1⅝in (4cm)

Cotton batting: cut 1 rectangle, 94½ x 25¼in (240 x 63cm)

Making the top

1 Place one wide and one narrow border piece right sides together, aligning their long edges. Pin, then machine stitch with a ⅝in (1.5cm) seam allowance. Repeat to join the other wide and narrow border pieces. Press the seams open.

2 With right sides together, align the narrower piece of the joined border with the short edge of the main fabric top. Pin in place along the edge.

3 Stitch together with a ⅝in (1.5cm) seam allowance. Repeat along the other short edge. Press each seam toward the border.

4 With the top face down, press back ¾in (2cm) at the end of the border. Fold the border so that its pressed edge aligns with the seam joining the top to the border. Press along this fold. Repeat for the other end.

Making and attaching the flat piping

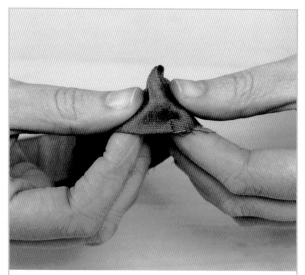

1 Fold each length of flat piping in half lengthwise, wrong sides together. Press. At the ends only, turn the piping right sides together. Stitch the ends closed with a ⅜in (1cm) seam allowance.

2 Turn each end to the right side, tucking the raw edges inside.

3 Lay the top face up. Starting at the fold line in the border, align the edge of the piping with the long edge of the top, as shown. Pin in place. Repeat along the other long edge.

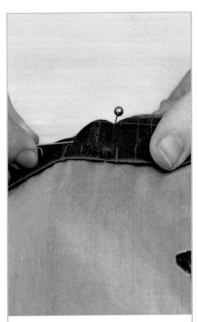

4 Baste (see p.18) the piping in place.

Assembling the runner

1 Fold the batting and the backing fabric in half widthwise to find the center points. Mark these with a pin at each edge.

2 Open out the batting and lay the backing fabric right side up on top, matching the center points. Smooth out any wrinkles from the backing fabric, working from the center outward.

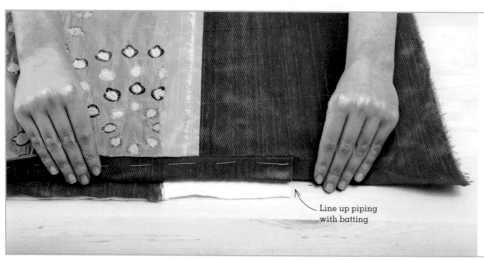

3 Place the runner top right side down on the backing, matching the raw edges. Align the end of the flat piping with the edge of the batting, as shown, ensuring that the edge of the batting lines up with the fold line in the border.

Line up piping with batting

4 Baste or pin all the layers together. Machine stitch along each long edge with a ⅝in (1.5cm) seam allowance, stopping and starting at the edge of the batting.

5 Turn the runner to the right side, then lay it on the work surface with the backing face up.

6 Fold over a ⅝in (1.5cm) seam allowance along the sides of the border, then fold and press a ⅝in (1.5cm) seam allowance along the end. Refold the ¾in (2cm) hem at the short end.

7 Fold the border along its fold line to meet the edge of the backing fabric. Pin in place.

8 Slip stitch (see p.18) the border in place, making sure not to stitch into the front of the runner. Repeat Steps 6–8 at the other end to finish.

Bean bag (pp.50–57)

Bean bag section
Enlarge by 500% on a photocopier

JOIN

Curtain tieback (pp.132–135)

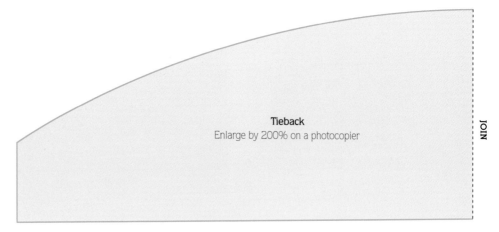

Tieback
Enlarge by 200% on a photocopier

JOIN

JOIN

Bean bag section
Enlarge by 500% on a photocopier

Bean bag top
Enlarge by 225% on a photocopier

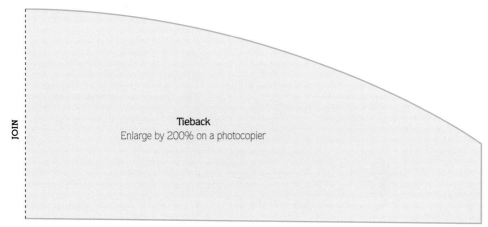

JOIN

Tieback
Enlarge by 200% on a photocopier

PUTTING IT
ALL TOGETHER

Using color and pattern

Using color and pattern is a great way to add style and personality to a room, but it's not as easy to get right as you might think. Follow our expert tricks below, though, and you'll create a successful theme effortlessly.

2 Keep a color scrapbook
Keep a record of colors and color combinations you like, as well as swatches of fabric or wallpapers that catch your eye. Then, when you want to add character to a room, you can use those as inspiration.

1 Where to start
When using pattern, first think about the size of your room and what you're trying to achieve. Do you want the room to feel cozy and intimate or bright and spacious? Lighter colors and larger prints will make a room feel more open, while deeper tones and smaller designs will create a warm and intimate feel.

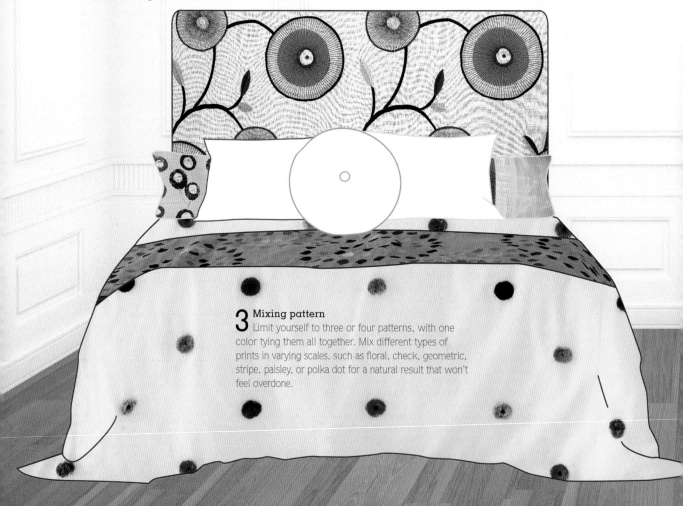

3 Mixing pattern
Limit yourself to three or four patterns, with one color tying them all together. Mix different types of prints in varying scales, such as floral, check, geometric, stripe, paisley, or polka dot for a natural result that won't feel overdone.

Ribbon ties →

5 Choosing a wall color

The main wall color will set the tone for the whole room, so if you're choosing paint, get exactly the right shade—a tone lighter or darker can make a difference. Buy samples of colors, paint large pieces of paper, and tack them onto the walls you're planning to paint. Then, see how the color looks in different lights.

4 Working together

Keep adjacent rooms in mind when decorating, and think about how the colors and patterns you are using will work together. They don't need to match—but they should harmonize or coordinate with other rooms—and shouldn't clash.

6 Add pattern in fabrics

Pillows and a rug are a great way to add instant color and pattern, and a patterned blind or curtains in an otherwise plain room will make your color scheme pop. Block colors create a lively contrast.

Ideas for small spaces

Make the most of a small room by being clever with your furniture and decorating choices. Every bit of space can be used to your advantage. Here's how.

3 Reflect space
A mirrored wall is a great way to open up a small space. The reflective surface creates an optical illusion of doubling the size of the space. It also picks up and reflects light from various sources in the room, especially at night.

1 Be clever with color
Painting walls in dark colors can make a room feel smaller, but used sparingly, you can still create a dramatic effect without the color dominating the room.

2 Choose folding furniture
A gateleg table can easily be stowed away or moved into another room. Folding chairs can be stored in a cupboard or turned into a feature by being hung on a wall when not in use.

4 Create space
Two armchairs offer a more versatile seating option than a sofa in a small room because you can move them around to create space when needed. Add a footstool so that you can stretch out.

5 Use lighting cleverly
Place lights at different levels to highlight various areas or features in the room, making it look intimate and cozy, or open and spacious.

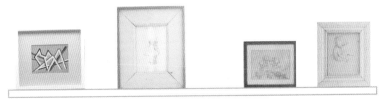

6 Install handy shelves

Shelves installed in unused spaces, such as above your bed, window, or door frames, provide extra storage for books and knickknacks, and are great for displaying pictures or mirrors, too.

8 Streamline your rooms

Swap bulky curtains for a more streamlined window dressing such as shutters or shades. This is also a great way to add color or pattern to a small room.

Light up dark corners

7 Fill wasted space

Use the space under the stairs to house a half bath, store coats and shoes, display a large object, or fill with shelves lined with storage boxes or baskets. Need a home office? It could fit here, too.

Use bold patterns as a feature

9 Use visual tricks

Wallpaper with vertical stripes or patterns can make a low-ceilinged room feel taller. Similarly, floor-to-ceiling cupboards make the most of space as well as creating the illusion of height. If you prefer plain walls, try floor-length curtains on poles set higher than the window to create a similar effect.

Creating light and airy spaces

Rooms that don't receive much natural light can feel dark and unwelcoming. While you might not be able to change the size of the room, you can transform it with these clever tricks to give it a light and airy feel.

1 Choose your wall color
As a general rule, the closer to white the paint, the more reflective it will be. Light colors such as pale gray, yellow, and blue make a room look larger, while darker colors make the room look smaller.

2 Use mirrors to reflect light
Placing a mirror adjacent to a window will reflect light around the room. The taller the mirror, the more effective the result and the higher the room's ceiling will feel.

Capture more light with a well-placed mirror

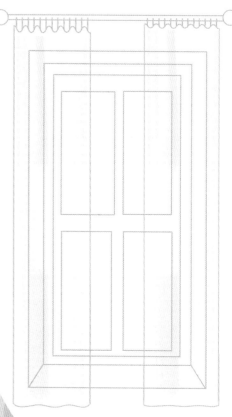

3 Avoid heavy, dark furniture
Instead, use pale wood, white painted, mirrored, acrylic plastic, or glass pieces that will reflect the light and appear to take up less space. Going for upholstered pieces? Choose light colors— just make sure the covers are easy to clean.

Light wood gives a spacious feeling

4 Hang sheer curtains
Curtains can absorb light, so swap heavy curtains for light or sheers. Fit a blackout roller shade or shutters behind the curtains if you need to block out artificial light at night, or need privacy at any time.

5 Choose high-gloss flooring
Hardwood and laminate, tiled, resin, and concrete flooring with a high-gloss finish will bounce light upward into a room, with lighter colors giving the best results.

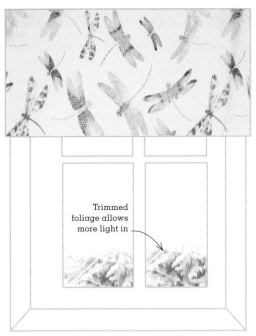

7 Declutter the space
Clutter absorbs light so keep surfaces as clear as possible. Only display what you really love, storing everything else away.

Keep sills free of clutter

Trimmed foliage allows more light in

6 Outside matters
Trim trees or bushes outside windows that could be keeping light from entering the room.

Glass makes the most of natural light

8 Swap the doors
Change solid interior doors for those with glazed panels. You could also consider putting a fanlight over a door.

Pale fabrics help to create a lighter look

9 Choose raised furniture
Dark, heavy furniture can absorb a lot of light. For a lighter feel, choose sofas and beds that have clear space underneath. If the floor is also a pale color, the light will bounce around the space, adding to the light, airy appearance of the room.

Finishing touches

Embellish your furnishings with colorful pillows and throws, and add a shade and tiebacks, too.

1 Add layers
A bedspread or blanket in either complementary or contrasting colors is a good opportunity to add some texture as well as color and pattern to your bed.

3 Swatches
Pin up a few swatches of fabric on the wall before you decide on color, pattern, and weight.

2 Add pillows
Finish by adding interest with pillows in both solid-colored and patterned fabrics. Pile on the pillows, and don't shy away from mixing patterns. Combine large prints with small ones, florals with geometrics.

5 Plants and flowers

A simple potted plant or flowers set on a coffee table, bookshelf, cabinet, or almost anywhere adds instant life and color.

Fresh flowers add color to any room

4 Seasonal changes

Use pillows, decorative objects, frames, and vases to make seasonal changes to your room. In summer, opt for fresh colors such as sky blue and yellow. In winter, swap them for purples and deep reds.

6 Curtain tiebacks

Tiebacks hold curtains away from the window, so that you get the maximum amount of light into the room. Make the tiebacks suit the length of the curtains.

7 Give it an edge

Adding a trim—lace, pom-pom, tassel, or beading—will instantly update pillows, curtains, hand towels, and lampshades. Use coordinating or contrasting colors.

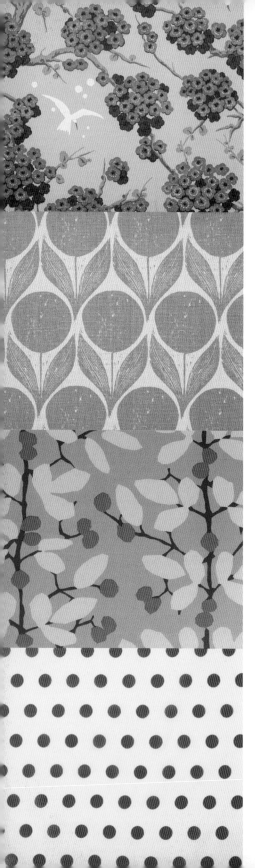

Fabric suppliers

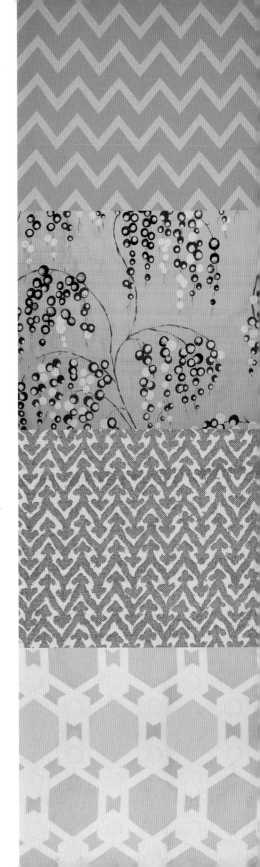

SUPPLIER WEBSITES

Bluebellgray: www.bluebellgray.com
Borovick Fabrics: www.borovickfabrics.com
Clarke & Clarke: www.clarke-clarke.co.uk
Fermoie: www.fermoie.com
Harlequin: www.harlequin.uk.com
Kirkby Design: www.kirkbydesign.com
Marimekko: www.marimekko.com
Osborne & Little: www.osborneandlittle.com
Romo: www.romo.com
Scion: www.scion.uk.com
Vanessa Arbuthnott: www.vanessaarbuthnott.co.uk
Villa Nova: www.villanova.co.uk
Voyage: www.voyagedecoration.com

Index

Acknowledgments

Contributors

DANIELLE BUDD AND BEVELEE JAY REGAN AT JAYWORKS

Danielle is a graduate of The Royal College of Art, specializing in printed textiles. Her degree show was a collection of unique handcrafted bags and purses, brought to life from her screen-printed leather and digital textile designs. Danielle went on to launch a successful accessories label, designed and made in-house and sold worldwide. She is currently a university lecturer in surface design at the University of the Arts, a freelance designer, and one half of Jayworks.

Bevelee has always been a sewing enthusiast and she has had a varied career in theater, styling, and merchandising. Bevelee went on to fine-tune her skills in advanced home furnishing at The Sir John Cass School of Furniture. Currently she is a furnishing tutor at Sew Over It, part of the merchandising team at Fabrics Galore, and is the other half of Jayworks.

Danielle and Bevelee have always been friends and are avid makers. Some years ago they decided to bring together their valuable knowledge and plethora of skills and launch Jayworks, a creative home furnishing company.

MIA PEJCINOVIC

Mia is a London-based freelance editorial and commercial stylist, as well as design consultant. For the past 15 years she has specialized in styling, set design, art direction, prop sourcing, and production for advertising, editorial, TV, and book publishing, and interior consultancy for residential clients in the UK and elsewhere.

Mia has worked on numerous exciting projects with some of the industry's most successful photographers. Her many clients include: Debbie Bliss, Designer Yarns, Mothercare, and Retreat Home; the magazines *Beautiful Kitchens*, *Country Homes & Interiors*, *Homes & Antiques*, *House Beautiful*, *Ideal Home*, *Image Interiors*, and *Real Homes*; and the UK TV show *The Hotel Inspector*.

Acknowledgments

Dorling Kindersley would like to thank the following people for their time, input, and expertise:

Photography assistants Emma Ercolani and Amy Barton
Hand models Alice Bowsher and Kate Meeker
Models Miriam Clarke, Ted Daley, Alice Bowsher, and Emma Ercolani
Illustrator Vanessa Hamilton for illustrations on pages 16, 17, 18, 19, 22, 23, 106, 107, 108, 109, 110, 111, 156, 157, and 190
Indexer Anne Hildyard
Additional pillows Gail Lockwood
Set builder Tim Warren
Locations for photography Light Locations and 1st Option
Prop rental Backgrounds Prop Hire